Three Horizons

Three Horizons

The Patterning of Hope

Second Edition

Bill Sharpe

First published: 2013
Second edition: 2020

Published by:
Triarchy Press
Axminster, UK

www.triarchypress.net

A catalogue record for this book is available from the British
Library.

ISBNs
Print: 978-1-911193-86-9
ePub: 978-1-911193-87-6
PDF: 978-1-911193-88-3

Artwork by Jennifer Williams

**Jennifer Williams is critically acclaimed at making hand-made
books, cut-outs, photographs, illustrations, prints and puppets.
She is a trustee and member of International Futures Forum and
for 31 years directed the Centre for Creative Communities.**

tp

Contents

Reviews of the First Edition i

Introduction v

PART I: THREE HORIZONS 1

    A Heated Conversation 3

    The Future in the Present 6

    The Three Horizons 9

    A Shared Future Consciousness 25

PART II: THE PRACTICE OF FUTURE CONSCIOUSNESS 29

    Seeing Everything as Patterns 31

    Putting Ourselves in the Picture 38

    Convening the Future: 49

    From Mindsets to Perspectives 49

PART III: JOURNEYS IN THREE HORIZONS 55

    Case Studies: Introduction 57

    Case Studies 62

    Case Studies: Summary 82

    Pushing out to Sea 85

PART IV: THE PATTERNING OF HOPE.. 87

    Knowing and Living....................................... 89

    Stepping into Future Consciousness............................ 95

    Hope 98

    Transformative Society................................. 102

    Navigating on the Open Sea......................... 107

Acknowledgements... 123

Notes.. 125

Bibliography... 131

REVIEWS of the First Edition

How can an eclectic group of experts, with very different worldviews, come to a shared vision for the future? Using the Three Horizons framework, skilled facilitators achieved the seemingly impossible and enabled the Carnegie Commission for Rural Community Development to agree a compelling, inspiring and hopeful blueprint for the future of rural communities. Now Bill Sharpe reveals the full potential for this way of thinking to generate practical hope in all kinds of complex policy areas.

Kate Braithwaite, Operations Director, UnLtd
and formerly Carnegie UK Trust

Every so often a new futures method comes along that opens up new ways of seeing the future. Three Horizons is such a method. It links the present to possible futures and embodies ways of identifying strategic and innovation challenges. Bill Sharpe, one of the Three Horizons pioneers, has written a valuable primer on its theory and emerging practice.

Andrew Curry, The Futures Company

Three Horizons provides a valuable tool for understanding the complexity hidden in past trends and the choices always implicit in the apparent determinism of future possibilities. An intelligent approach to seeing into the future demands both insight into the underlying forces driving surface events and the imagination to know that what appears self-evident may be only the result of a pattern of logic that fails to take fully into account the future play of those forces. Bill Sharpe's book helps us break out of the Newtonian deterministic thinking that so often blinds us to the choices we have made and reveals our power to alter them.

Garry Jacobs, Chairman and CEO of
the World Academy of Arts and Sciences

We need to pass from worrying about the future to constructively engaging upon its creation. For all those interested in this task, this book delivers a powerful way of thinking about that future in qualitatively different horizons. If we want transformation to be more than just an aspiration, then we need to position it and to understand the dilemmas that define progress towards a better society. This book helps with that positioning and puts discipline into the process of foresight.

Professor Peter Kawalek, Manchester Business School

...we encourage occupational scientists to embrace the Three Horizons (Sharpe, 2013), a simple and intuitive framework for thinking about the future and how to bring about positive change.

Developed over several years by members of the International Futures Forum, this framework creates an awareness of the future potential of the present, a "future consciousness" (Sharpe, 2013, p. 8), enabling a mindset to create a future that society needs and wants.

... The Three Horizons framework has been used effectively by various groups to create transformative change and innovation (Sharpe, 2013, pp.65–85). According to Sharpe, transformative change results from re-patterning the way people do things rather than merely extending current patterns. Given the nature of the wicked problems impacting on population health, we believe occupational scientists need to investigate ways and means of initiating transformative change as their contribution to research on the uncertain future that lies ahead. We believe that to tackle wicked problems such as climate change, occupational scientists and others need to do research differently and re-conceptualise the future. The Three Horizons framework can assist in enabling members of research teams to start conversations about innovative ways of creating a transformed future."

Dr Alison Wicks and Dr Maggie Jamieson in
Journal of Occupational Science

Three Horizons is more than a tool to describe the Litany of change. It's also a way to surface different perspectives on an issue in a very overt way, and to move beyond those seemingly intractable perspectives to collaborative ways of thinking about possible futures, or 'holding transformational dialogue which informs our action in the complexity of the present while respecting the unknowability of the future...

Like all frameworks, the Three Horizons is only useful and relevant if it fits the context in which one is working and living. So far, I've found it useful in different ways in client contexts and in my own scanning as a way to map out the scope of change being faced. The Three Horizons is not just a tool for understanding change and transformation though. It's also a way to understand the power of intent and hope—individual and collective—as we look towards the future.

And like all things transformational and developmental, once the Three Horizons is understood and embedded in thinking and working, there's no going back."

Maree Conway, Founding Partner: The Centre for Australian Foresight, writing in The Association of Professional Futurists' *Compass* Newsletter.

'Three Horizons: The Patterning of Hope' by Bill Sharpe is a tremendous book for anyone who works on profound change. ...My key takeaway: rather than aiming for distant, definitive visions, we would be better to act from a shared awareness of the future potential in this present moment.

Last autumn I read 'Three Horizons', at the suggestion of Forum for the Future's Director of Futures, James Goodman. Thank goodness I did. Few books have resonated with me as much on the overwhelming messiness of profound, social change. In a time of Trump and Brexit, and of us still driving climate change even though we are putting civilisation at risk, it gave me hope and it gave shifted my modus operandi.

David Bent, Social entrepreneur and consultant to the UK Cabinet Office

INTRODUCTION

Over the last few years I have found myself in many discussions with people who are wrestling with problems of daunting complexity. Sometimes, when tasked with producing a report, I would struggle to find a way to write something that was both useful and which respected our collective ignorance of what to do. Gradually it has dawned on me that we lack good ways to work with unknowing, to respect lack of knowledge but work skilfully with it. All the tools that make up the field of futures and foresight work – and that should be appropriate for this task – seem to fall short. We don't even have a good word for not knowing – 'ignorance' certainly doesn't do it, suggesting as it does that we haven't taken the time to find out what we could. If I asked for good things to read about ignorance, people laughed.

I slowly came to realise that, in the emerging practice of Three Horizons, we had discovered something useful. Here was a simple framework that seemed to allow us to work with what we know at the same time as engaging creatively with what we do not know. Instead of having to build afresh, for each new project, a way to think about the future, we had in our hands a simple way to structure the discussion that would hold the complexity in a productive way and enable us to work with it. More than that, it allowed us to work with our own response to the challenge, to come together in exploring our visions, to make of hope not only an individual capacity not to give up, but a way to respond with creativity towards the not yet known.

Three Horizons is a way of working with change; it is a foresight tool. It is helpful for this because of the way it naturally turns towards systemic patterns rather than individual events or unexamined trends; it frames our discussion in terms of the shift from the established patterns of the first horizon to the emergence of new patterns in the third, via the transition activity of the

second. Beyond this orientation to patterns, the central idea of Three Horizons, and what makes it so useful, is that it draws attention to the three horizons as existing always in the present moment, and that we have evidence about the future in how people (including ourselves) are behaving *now*. By making these qualitative distinctions between the three horizons in the present, a lot of dynamics of change come into view quite naturally, and we are led to explore them in terms of the patterns of behaviour of those who are maintaining or creating them. This leads to the third benefit, that we can reflect on our own intentions towards those patterns in the process of exploring the behaviour and intent that is revealed in each horizon.

So, from this simple framework we have got three things: we have a way to look at the processes of change that encourages to see deeper patterns of behaviour beneath surface events; we have made the future accessible in the present in the form of the intent and actions that are bringing it about; and we find that we are naturally bringing all the voices of continuity and change into play as part of the discussion, as expressed in their intent towards the patterns.

Over the last few years this way of working on complex problems has taken on a life of its own. Many people have started using the Three Horizons framework as a way to work on their issues. Talking to some of the people who have been using it has confirmed this understanding of why it works. All of them spoke of the way it separates things out in a helpful way and improves the dialogue, because people can see where they are and can avoid unnecessary confusion and conflict between the three horizons. Another benefit is that Three Horizons can be used without a big investment in what might be thought of as a 'futures' project. It turns out to be quite natural, in almost any situation where people are working on some complex issue, to gently bring out the three 'voices' of the horizons: the managerial voice that is concerned with the first horizon responsibility for keeping things going; the entrepreneurial voice of the second horizon that is eager to get on and try new things (some of which won't work); and the aspiration and vision of the third horizon voice that holds out for commitment to a better way and the opportunity that can be imagined in the mind's eye.

Seeing this success it was natural to think about spreading Three Horizons more widely by writing a book and cultivating the further understanding of the practice of using it. This has turned out to be surprisingly difficult, but the difficulties point to the deeper potential of this simple tool. It is rather as if, having discovered that a stick and some coloured liquid can make marks on a piece of bark, we suddenly get an inkling of what might become possible if we all learned to write. A whole new world of thought seems to come into view, but to get there needs some big strides, like the development of literacy that changed how thought is expressed and shared between us. This is what happened as I took on the simple task of writing down what Three Horizons is as a futures tool. I have seen coming into view a much greater potential for us to express our shared intent towards the future in much more powerfully productive ways. I have found myself working on a third horizon vision of transformation, in which we will be able to hold together a more resilient solidarity in the face of the complex challenges confronting us.

This book is a first attempt to express both the simplicity at the heart of Three Horizons and what it might lead to. I have, with some presumption, called this emerging practice 'future consciousness' to flag up the scale of the ambition that it represents. I am hoping that this term might help us to become reflectively aware of our experience so that we can build a widely shared practice in transformational change in conditions of uncertainty.

The book takes you on the same journey that my colleagues and I have been on in coming to this point. In Part I there is a basic description of Three Horizons as it can apply to any issue when you want to take a longer term perspective and explore possibilities for transformational change. It also sets the scene for the exploration of the underlying practice of future consciousness in the rest of the book. In Part II I have reflected on my own experience, and that of other practitioners I have worked closely with, to start identifying the underlying practice that makes Three Horizons 'work'. My hope in doing this is to start a process of further reflection and learning amongst all practitioners, so that my experience can be challenged and improved by that of others. Part III is a fairly self-contained group of accounts of the use of Three Horizons in IFF projects that illustrate some of the different ways it can be used. These accounts have been written by Graham Leicester and Andrew Lyon of IFF.

Finally, in Part IV I have given myself the freedom to write in a more speculative way about the vision of what future consciousness might be. It is this that gives the book its subtitle, *the patterning of hope*, and it is this that has made the book so hard to write. However, in wrestling with that difficulty I have realised that I am living in my own personal version of a Three Horizons challenge – trying to provide a neat, first horizon description of this emerging practice and the simple tool that supports it, while holding true to the possibilities of a third horizon vision that can only be reached in collaboration with everyone else.

The four parts of the book can be taken as four essays around this theme of how we work with the known while responding creatively and skilfully together to the unknown. This is not a 'how to' manual for doing a Three Horizons project – references are provided for material currently available for that. Rather, it is offered as a contribution to the patterning of hope for all our futures.

PART I:
THREE HORIZONS

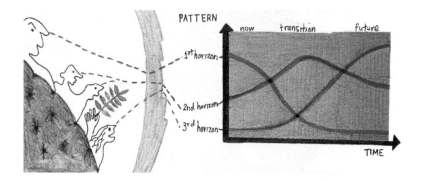

A Heated Conversation

When something occurs that gives us pause for thought about our present circumstances we tend to start a conversation about the future. Somebody might have presented us with a tempting opportunity. Or a colleague might have been 'let go' during hard times. Or we might have read a report on climate change suggesting recent weird weather patterns are a sign of things to come.

These snippets of information or experience make us question the present pattern of our lives. Our minds naturally fill with thoughts about possible future consequences. Should I take a chance and grasp the opportunity? What if I am next in line for the sack? Might it be time to start taking climate change seriously? What is naturally stirring in us is what I call our 'future consciousness'.

We can see it stirring in group settings too, although it is rarely acknowledged. Imagine the following conversation, typical of what might take place in the Boardroom of an education department or agency about the enduring connection between poor economic and social circumstances and poor educational performance.

The depressing statistics are presented, going back over several decades. In spite of countless initiatives, the correlation between poverty and poor educational performance seems as solid as ever. It is not long before the Chairman voices a thought that many around the table are having. "Inequality is an intractable issue", he says. "The link between poverty and poor attainment has been with us for generations. I really think we will still be here in ten years' time discussing exactly the same issue."

To some this sounds defeatist. A Board member with more recent experience in the classroom points to telling examples of small-scale projects which she knows have made a real difference.

"If we had less hand-wringing and more action we could get behind these projects... and invent others. Of course the gap can be closed."

This prompts a third person to speak up. "It is simply intolerable", she says, "that in the 21st century, in a wealthy nation like ours, the circumstances of your birth still count for so much. I don't think we can hold our heads up as a national agency effectively perpetuating a system in which poverty is fate. It is time to stand up and be counted."

A passionate discussion ensues, ebbing backwards and forwards between the voice of concern ("I really can't see things improving"), the voice of enterprise ("there must be something we can try") and the voice of aspiration ("if we can imagine a world of radical equality then surely we can build it"). The perspectives seem incompatible. Accusations fly, particularly against the voice of aspiration, which is felt to be at odds with the real world. "If you really believe that's possible, I want some of the pills you're taking."

Eventually, as lunch draws near, the Chairman brings the discussion to a close. He has been surprised by the passion released and a little concerned by the deep tensions the conversation has revealed. But he has not himself been persuaded to shift from his long-held view that when it comes to educational attainment, poverty is indeed fate and no amount of 'innovation' in the system will make any real difference.

Even so, he senses that something must be done, if only to maintain cohesion in the Board. So he duly records an intention to commission more detailed research into the causes of the problem, and to engage a specialist futures consultancy in a scenarios project in order to get a better handle on the long-term future. Passions subside and the Board moves on to the next agenda item: HR.

It is the contention of this book that the group did not need to engage a futures consultancy to have a conversation about the future. They were already having one. The strongly held views

expressed were in fact different perspectives on the future potential of the present moment. Most such conversations naturally reveal three dominant perspectives. The Chairman has presided over the growing success of the dominant system but now sees nothing but trouble ahead. The entrepreneur senses in this the scope for new thinking, new ideas, new approaches and wants to try something different. The visionary, increasingly impatient with both views, wants to make a stand and press for radical action.

These positions correspond in our framework to three horizons – three possible patterns in which the present might play out into the future. All three are always present, in any conversation and indeed in our own thinking. Being able to identify them and work skilfully with them, in groups, communities, nations, and within ourselves, is a practice that we can all develop. It restores our sense of agency in the face of a future that is, and always has been, radically open. We call this Three Horizons thinking – in the service of the conscious practice of 'future consciousness'.

The Future in the Present

How can people work together to create transformational change in the face of the uncertain future? There are two main sorts of change – that which continues the pattern of how we are doing things today, and that which starts a new pattern. A caterpillar grows by getting longer and fatter, but this can only go on for a while before it reaches the limit. The caterpillar cannot turn into a butterfly by eating more, taking exercise, or anything else – it has to go through a transformation in how it is organised and how it relates to the world around it. The caterpillar changes the pattern of its life, abandoning the old and adopting the new. Similarly, we recognise the need for transformational change when we see that the way things are getting done now has limits; that we cannot get beyond these limits however much we try to improve the existing system, and that we must, as a result, create a new pattern of life for the future we want and need.

A caterpillar 'knows' what it has to become, its path of transformation is mapped out for it, but transformation for us is a process of exploration, and to explore we must travel over the horizon towards the unknown. We can only see the world from where we are: we may be on a beach or at the top of a mountain, but wherever we stand, the world that we can see gradually gives way to the horizon of sight. As our direct perception fails so our knowledge and imagination must take over. Perhaps some people have explored a little way and come back with stories of what they have seen, or perhaps there are high mountains peeping over the horizon and rivers flowing from them that carry clues to what lies beyond. If we are happy where we are, and have no need to travel, such speculation can stay as day dreams, but if we want to set out to new lands we must use these fragments to equip ourselves for an unpredictable journey over the horizon to an envisioned destination. We can only learn more by setting out on the

journey; we must choose a direction and be ready to learn and adapt as we go.

When we have to act to realise our intentions in a complex and uncertain world, we are faced with the same problem: the familiar way of doing things is all around us, but gradually gives way to a future that lies over the horizon of what we can know. We can see change and innovation going on, we can look for signs in the present of the deeper trends that will shape events, and we can envision the future that we hope can be reached. But if we are to get anywhere we have to choose our direction and set off, unsure of what we will find, guided by a blend of knowledge, imagination and our values.

Three Horizons is a way to think about the future that recognises deep uncertainty but responds with an active orientation; that allows us to understand more clearly how our actions and those of others we engage with might shape the future we are trying to explore. This is especially important when we look at issues of broad societal concern, where we are all, as members of society, actors in the future. In these cases we are particularly concerned to find ways for the many different constituencies in society to come together to unlock the future from the dominance of old ways of doing things – ways that are no longer working for us.

Three Horizons thinking offers a way to find and shape our own intentions more clearly as we look over the first horizon of the known towards the second and third horizons of innovation and transformation towards the future. It transforms the potential of the present moment by revealing each horizon as a different quality of the future in the present, reflecting how we act differently to maintain the familiar or pioneer the new. The outcome of Three Horizons work is a map of transformational potential which enables us to act with more skill, freedom and creativity in the present, both individually and together. There are two constituencies for such work: those who act as players in each horizon within the patterns and those whose ability to set policy and govern can enable or disable the actions of the players.

The foundation of the Three Horizons approach is that it is well aligned with three natural forms of awareness which everybody can adopt towards the future and quite easily describe. By default, many people inhabit just one horizon in their work, and view other horizons with varying degrees of perplexity, misunderstanding or hostility – like the Chairman in the little cameo above. However, everyone has a natural capacity to work with the other horizons, and the core of Three Horizons practice is the flexibility to work with all three modes of awareness. As people make this step individually they can also make it together – developing a shared culture of future consciousness that in turn opens up a greater freedom of action. This deeper, collective awareness is itself a third horizon vision – a future consciousness of transformational capacity for everyone.

THE THREE HORIZONS

A simple linear view of change places us in the present moment looking towards how we want things to be in future, and it typically divides time into now, the midterm and long-term future. That way of thinking places the future as outside the present moment, seen only as something that might or might not happen, and makes it appear in the guise of the unknown or unknowable and the risky. Yet we act with future intent all the time, linking what we are doing today to some future outcome, and it is helpful to see that we do this naturally in three quite distinct ways. These are in fact different ways not only of looking at the future but of bringing it into being, and so they are three ways of relating the future to our actions in the present.

We can represent these three relationships of the present to the future as three horizons which describe a pattern of change over time in our area of interest, as shown in the picture at the beginning of this section.

The first horizon describes the current way of doing things, and the way we can expect it to change if we all keep behaving in the ways we are used to. H1 systems are what we all depend on to get things done in the world. Throughout the day we make use of a myriad societal systems – shops, schools, banks, hospitals, transport – and most of the time we don't want, or need, to think about them too much; we all help perpetuate the system by taking part in it. While we talk a lot about the pace of chance, it is worth remembering that lots of things must stay the same for daily life to go on. Innovation and change in our H1 systems is happening, but it is about sustaining and extending the way things are done now in a planned and orderly way; uncertainties and risks are to be eliminated or prepared for – the lights must be kept on.

Nothing lasts forever, and over time we inevitably find that our H1 ways of doing things are falling short – no longer meeting expectations, failing to move towards new opportunities, or out of step with emerging conditions. More than that, we have a sense that our H1 methods of improvement and innovation do not ever get us where we want to go and are just sustaining the old approach with its failings; that approach is losing its 'fitness for purpose'.

The third horizon is the future system. It is those new ways of living and working that will fit better with the emerging need and opportunity. H3 change is transformative, bringing a new pattern into existence that is beyond the reach of the H1 system. There will be many competing visions of the future and early pioneers are likely to look quite unrealistic – and some of them are. As we build our own Three Horizons map we bring our own vision to bear and take a view on how it relates to the visions of others and the trends that are playing out for all of us.

The second horizon is the transition and transformation zone of emerging innovations that are responding to the shortcomings of the second horizon and anticipating the possibilities of the third horizon. New ways of doing things emerge in messy ways, brought about through some combination of deliberate action and opportunistic adaptation in the light of circumstances. Entrepreneurs must judge the moment, and bring together ideas and resources to try a new way of doing things here and now. They live in an ambiguous territory where the old ways are dominant but the new is becoming possible; they can look to the past and fit in with familiar patterns of life, or try to become the seed that grows into the new. Entrepreneurship is hard and most attempts to do new things fail; it is much easier to serve the old systems, and established H1 players typically dominate.

The foundation of the Three Horizons approach is to explore the future as the interaction between the three horizons. We seek to understand all the actors, including ourselves, in terms of the role they play in sustaining H1 systems or bringing about transitions and transformations in the second and third horizons. We cast this as a process of competition between the first horizon and the third horizon that is played out in the ambiguous territory of the second horizon.

Three Horizons is a spatial metaphor – it moves the process of change over time into a simple diagram in space on the page. It combines the notion of time moving from left to right with the idea of change as the interplay of the three horizons, moving from the dominance of the familiar to the emergence of the new. Once we start to see our concerns through the idea of patterns of activity that are continuously growing, changing, living and dying, it becomes easier to understand the dynamics of change. We see each horizon as describing a distinct type of behaviour that is either maintaining an existing pattern or starting a new one that may flourish or die, and we see that all patterns are always in motion, interacting, and sensitive to changing conditions.

All three horizons are always present, and each horizon is a way of acting in the present moment with a future-oriented intent – a way that is characterised by a distinctive mindset. The H1 mindset is managerial and is about maintaining the system or innovating within it without taking risks with its integrity. The dominant H2 attitude is entrepreneurial – seeing and grasping the opportunities that it offers. The H3 outlook is visionary and aspirational; it is about setting out to make something happen even if it is at odds with current knowledge and values.

We can become aware of the three horizons as three distinct qualities of the present moment – three different potentials for action that relate the present to the future in distinct ways, each unfolding over time in its own way, and all interacting in the process of change. These three qualities of the present are all quite natural and familiar to us, but we have not necessarily become aware of them or of the choices and freedoms that become available to us when we use them to work together on change.

This is the core idea of Three Horizons: to shift from our simple, one-dimensional view of time stretching into the future and instead adopt a three-dimensional view in which we are aware of each horizon as a distinct quality of relationship between the future and the present. We call the move into this multi-dimensional view, and the skill to work with it, the step into *future consciousness*.

Transformation happens as the emergent result of everything going on in the world – there is always an emerging third horizon at every scale of life from the individual to the planet and beyond. Some things will be the result of conscious intent, others will surprise us for good or ill. The way we live now was once the third horizon, partly imagined and intended, largely unknown. Future consciousness will not bring the future under control, but allows us to develop our capacity for a transformational response to its possibilities.

In the remainder of this part we look at the three horizons in more detail. Although the logical order might seem to be to move from the first horizon through the second to the third, instead we go from the first to the third. The second horizon is where tensions and transitions are played out between the continuous improvement of H1 and the transformational possibilities of H3 and can only be properly understood when we hold them both in mind. This one-three-two ordering is also the way to use the three horizons in practice.

THE FIRST HORIZON –

TODAY'S DOMINANT PATTERN

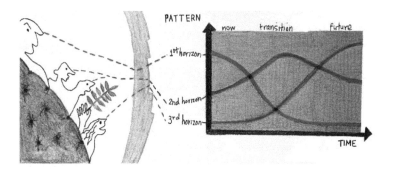

To be a living thing, like a tree or a person, is to grow into a particular relationship with the local context. We grow up, learn a particular language, train for a particular career, invest in a house, and so on. Each choice embeds a life effectively where it finds itself, and the positive benefits of such embedding are known as the effect of 'increasing returns'. A tree puts down its roots which draw up more water and nutrients, and grows its branches to put out more leaves which capture more light, and so it can grow deeper roots and bigger branches; the tree gets increasing returns from its own growth which it uses for further growth. Likewise, the better you become at your job the more you get opportunities for experience and promotion, and so you improve more, in a virtuous cycle.

However, the more closely and effectively we relate to our present conditions, the more we may experience a cost of adaptation if the situation changes. You can move a sapling and it will recover, but it is very hard to move a fully grown tree. I may have to retrain if my job goes away, learn a new language if I choose to emigrate, and so on, and this might set me back a long

way. All living things must make a trade-off between being well-adapted to live a particular life and having capabilities to adapt to a new one. At some point the cost of change is beyond what can be accomplished by an individual and change has to be carried forward by someone else. Thus no one organism lives for ever, but the species as a whole changes through adaptive processes that produce new individuals who take advantage of new conditions; this is the process of evolution.

Similarly with our societal organisations, there is an unavoidable choice between building up resources in doing something well under current conditions, and having the capacity to change to meet new circumstances. Once we are committed to one approach we invest all sorts of resources in perpetuating it: we design things in certain ways, we learn over many generations to make them better and cheaper, we learn appropriate skills, and so on. The law of increasing returns means that even if several ways of doing things are in principle as good as each other, once one of them is chosen it rapidly becomes much better than the others as resources are devoted to it. For example, of all the saplings that colonise a clearing in the wood one or two get slightly ahead of the others, start to capture more light, use this to grow faster, and become the new tall trees in that place, capturing all the resources.

Our H1 way of doing things is supported by the H1 frame of mind we all bring to it, which regards it as the settled way things are done around here. With our H1 mindset, with all our accumulated experience and resources, we look ahead and extend the current pattern out into the future as far as we can see, expecting, as with the real horizon, that as we move ahead our space of opportunity will continue to expand towards it. This is the manner of thinking that regards the current way of doing things as entirely appropriate to emerging conditions as long as we keep extending and developing it. For example, in transport this is found in the longstanding policy approach known as 'predict and provide'. Forecasts are made of demand for capacity,

roads and airports are built, and the forecast growth occurs, which generates more demand, for which forecasts are made and so on. Within this approach to framing policy development there is no way to explore what changes might be made within the wider social context that would constrain the unlimited demand for transport growth in ways that might help alleviate other problems such as pollution.

H1 systems of production and use have had time to permeate the whole of society and operate within settled societal rights, rules and norms of behaviour. Some of these H1 systems are so important to society that they achieve the status of 'infrastructure', meaning that their continued integrity is a concern of government, such as energy, telecommunications, transport and so on. Others, while primarily commercial, are nonetheless so important to us that their interests are closely entwined with our lives and livelihoods, with the result that vested interests play a large part in policy making.

H1 systems are fully integrated with the surrounding culture, and this means that there are some well-established ways of dealing with questions, issues and problems. So, any emerging challenge or constraint is framed according to the capabilities and possibilities of these H1 systems. The most efficient way to handle new problems or potentialities is usually to extend the old – never underestimate the power of the existing system to reach further than it has before. On the positive side, this means that incremental change can be brought about in efficient ways without disrupting too much how things are being done now. On the negative side, society can suffer from 'regulatory capture' when vested interests are able to control change to serve their own needs and prevent change that would have wider benefit.

For example, one of the liveliest areas of policy dispute in recent years has been in media and how they should be protected. With the rise of the World Wide Web it has become easy for material to be shared and distributed, supporting completely new ways for us all to collaborate and build on each other's

contributions. This has created huge problems for the long-established publishers and owners of content. They are finding it very difficult to adapt to the new realities and have mostly spent their energy fighting the change through arguing for the tightening and extending of old laws rather than finding creative ways to adapt to, and benefit from, the new possibilities.

We commonly describe the Horizon 1 systems as 'locked in' to emphasise the strength of their hold on resources and their resistance to change. Like a living organism, the social pattern re-applies resources to perpetuate and reproduce itself and fend off attacks from competitors. For new systems to arise they must not only be better adapted to emerging conditions but must somehow get established in the presence of today's dominant systems that are commanding all the resources: it is like trying to get new flowers growing in a garden overrun with bracken and brambles.

This resistance is not necessarily bad, it is often the result of good people working to maintain the effective functioning of the things we rely on – after all, today's first horizon was once the future, the third horizon of a previous era – it only becomes a problem when it no longer fits the emerging conditions, and then the inability to adapt locks up the resources needed by the new.

THE THIRD HORIZON –

THE FUTURE PATTERN

The third horizon is the landscape of new ways of doing things that will arise from changing conditions, new knowledge and new societal priorities and values.

In principle we can make radically different choices about values and rights, and how they govern our patterns of life, but in practice the momentum of the first horizon will lead to extensions of its own systems and make it hard, if not impossible, to create transition paths that challenge them. To make this concrete we will do a quick thought experiment.

Imagine that human evolution had happened in the absence of fossil fuels, or that they were only present in moderate amounts such that they could not have been the source of energy for an industrial revolution, but only as a useful feedstock for manufacturing processes. What would have happened? What would the history of science and technology look like? Would an industrial revolution have happened? Would it have been delayed? If all the societal investment that has gone into our existing energy systems had instead gone into non-fossil fuel alternatives, is there any reason to suppose that advanced economies such as ours could not have developed and had the characteristics of growth that we take for granted?

It seems quite easy to imagine that the growing civilisation on such a planet, when it needed to find a source of energy, would have looked around at the wind, sun, tides, and concluded that there was plenty of energy available (a small percentage of sunlight reaching the Earth would be enough). Just as we are now assuming that we can develop renewable energy technologies with sufficient application of science and engineering, these could have been developed first, with all the benefits to those technologies that come from being the primary application of societal resources.

However, here on Earth we are struggling to create the transition pathways from fossil fuel dependence to sustainable energy futures. The fossil fuel H1 systems have had many generations of evolution and so it is very hard to establish renewables as competitive alternatives. And around the basic energy industries there are many other systems that have co-evolved to use fossil fuel energy, such as the electricity grid, motor vehicles and so on, each one presenting problems of transition. The energy system we can imagine does not fit the present infrastructure.

The problem of energy transition presents very particular challenges, but the problem is more general: whenever we look ahead we see a future shaped by the extension of past decisions. Those futures that could be imagined, but which are radically at odds with current social norms and locked-in systems, seem unreachable and fanciful and are, in fact, very hard to conceive and reach. They are hard to think about because there is not a deep body of expertise available, and they are hard to reach because the dynamics of H1 systems work against them. As we noted before, this inbuilt conservatism is not in itself necessarily bad; we are all quite glad that the mad visionary is going to have a hard time winning the case for some radically unpredictable and potentially harmful innovation. Incremental progress allows our established institutions to adapt, making best use of tried and tested ways of handling things.

A Three Horizon process brings the third horizon possibilities into the present. This allows us to see whether we are genuinely exploring possibilities of transformational action or are being trapped within H1 assumptions of incremental improvement. To find H3 futures we must systematically explore the full range of possible social settlements and systems that could be brought into being. While we stay within our H1 thinking we are likely to remain silent about the underlying cultural assumptions on

which it is based and maintain the fiction that we are studying uncertainties and emerging trends in an objective way. But H3 thinking must explicitly bring those assumptions to light and question them. This is creative work for the imagination, loosening our thoughts from the familiar way things are, exploring how they might be, and being open to all sorts of new ideas whether we agree with them or not.

The Three Horizons framework invites us to become aware of who the 'we' are in the previous paragraph. Who is doing the exploration, how are we convening the discussion and what responsibility for action are we assuming in those present? It builds our intent, and that of others, naturally into the process. There is no presumption that everyone will agree on the vision of the third horizon, but it is a step forward to clarify whether discussions are between competing visions of the third horizon or a conflict between the first horizon and the third. By uncovering the assumptions and values that are in play we can approach the task of transformation as convening a conversation of interests.

Exploring the third horizon is a skill in working creatively with the unknown, the partially known and the uncertain. It is a skill we all have, but have not fully developed as a collective capacity of transformation. It is the subject of the rest of this book. But first we look at the second horizon, where the dynamics of transition are played out.

THE SECOND HORIZON –

AMBIGUOUS INNOVATION

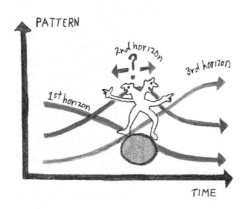

H2 thinking looks both ways and is inherently ambiguous. Changing circumstances present us with constraints and new opportunities. Should we meet them with old ways of doing things or new? What does this choice mean? Does our legitimacy come from the old world view or the new? And who gets to decide?

The second horizon is the zone of innovation, where new ways of doing things are appearing that are responding to the limitations of the first horizon and the opportunity of the third. Innovation is the process that takes an idea and assembles the resources needed to establish it in the world. For a business, that means finding financial investors who can see a possibility of a return for their capital; for a social enterprise it might be more about recruiting support from charitable institutions and policy makers to tackle an old problem in a new way; for a producer in the arts it is taking the risk of finding resources to introduce something new to an audience.

Many innovations fail – the new business does not catch on, the innovative social policy does not continue beyond its pilot experiment or the artistic vision has no impact. The second horizon is a zone of experimentation where society allows new things to be tried, but only some go on to become established. How this happens, of course, varies greatly across different areas of life and different cultures: market economies are built to support innovation whereas some sorts of social organisation actively suppress it.

H2 innovation when it succeeds will frequently 'disrupt' the H1 systems, displacing them from their central role and occupying the new centre ground. It is common to find that the old H1 systems do not disappear, but have to move into a secondary role in the new order of things, in the way that railways were displaced by roads as our dominant mode of personal transport, for example. It is the nature of H2 innovation that it is full of uncertainty over who will win, who will lose, what standards will emerge, what people will accept and reject, and so on.

As an H2 innovation gains a foothold it starts to become embedded in society, and gradually builds up new distributions of power between producers and users, and creates new interest groups with positions to protect. As an innovation is taken up into more and more uses so it locks in many interests in its continuation. Once an innovation starts down this path, it benefits from the allocation of resources to its continuation through the effect of increasing returns, and so gains a rapidly increasing advantage over other alternatives that were competing for attention.

Although we are accustomed to thinking of innovation as being about pioneering the new, we have already seen that the H1 innovation can trap us in incremental improvement that holds us back from the third horizon. Paradoxically, in important respects, H2 innovation is also biased towards the past not the future. First, most resources for doing new things are in the hands of the H1 providers. So, they will generally try to co-opt new possibilities to extend their own positions. Governments will often actively support this co-option, either because the system is an infrastructure and their responsibility is to 'keep the lights on' or because they have no particular reason to challenge the incumbents and their view of the future. In the worst case, they continue to support, and even subsidise, H1 players just because of those players' special interest power over the political process.

So, for instance, we are currently seeing the content industry (those who own books, films and so on) promoting very vigorous extensions of content protection legislation into the digital realm, opposed by people promoting the third horizon value enabled by the Web of a much stronger 'cultural commons' for everyone.

Another, and not so obvious, bias of H2 innovation towards the first horizon is that it is much easier to innovate within existing systems of societal rights and norms than to have to challenge them; to continue the digital media example, those innovators who challenged the H1 norms head on by pioneering peer-to-peer file sharing to distribute free music were heavily suppressed by the incumbents, with the support of the legal system. By contrast, Steve Jobs skilfully established the iPod within the H1 norm of people paying for music downloads, but also published an article saying that Apple was content to embrace the move towards free music, keeping options open for the move to the third horizon.

Finally, H2 innovation is biased towards the past because governments, as well as supporting the integrity of H1 systems, are rightly very wary of interfering too closely in the process of innovation. A new system takes time to become established and it has to find a niche where it has distinctive advantages over the old. By definition, this cannot meet the needs that the mainstream infrastructure is supporting, even though over time it may gradually do so. So governments often find they have no straightforward way of introducing the new in the presence of the old. As a result they can support the processes of innovation

– by supporting research and pilot programmes – but have to leave the selection and exploitation of these programmes to market-based systems. But these systems, as we have seen, are historically biased in their underlying assumptions concerning rights and resources, and these positions are defended by the dominant players in the first horizon, so government policies will often result in creating new knowledge resources that will be exploited within those assumptions by those who will benefit from them, rather than challenging those assumptions.

We refer to this phenomenon of the first horizon absorbing the potential of H2 innovation as 'H1 capture', and the H2 innovations that result as 'H2 minus' (H2-) behaviour. This is one of the major impediments to transformative change. On the forward-looking side of the second horizon are the H2+ innovations that are taking us towards the third horizon. Hybrid cars are an example of this. Electric cars have many limitations on range and speed, so fully electric vehicles are a difficult proposition to bring to market. Hybrid vehicles, such as the Toyota Prius, blend the old and new technologies into a single package. The owner benefits from more efficient fuel consumption and Toyota benefits from the increasing returns of deploying and learning about electric vehicle technologies. At this stage the hybrid vehicles have no need for electricity charging points, but as such infrastructure becomes available the transition to fully electric vehicles will be a smooth one for the manufacturer.

Governments can sometimes foster H2+ innovations through standards, which signal a direction for innovation and foster competition. The German government helped its renewable industry flourish by its early use of payments for electricity delivered into the grid from renewable sources (so called 'Feed-In Tariffs'). This created incentives for innovation in renewable energy while also fostering competition between the various technologies.

Unfortunately there is no easy way to decide how to foster the forward-looking H2+ over the backward-pulling H2-. Hybrid cars have lower fuel consumption, and their owners may use that advantage to drive further for the same cost. Congestion charging that exempts such vehicles may therefore have the perverse effect of causing people to travel further. This analysis is not for or against hybrids or congestion charging, it is just intended to point out that there are no general rules. The advantage of mapping an issue with Three Horizons is that it can help reveal this ambiguity between the plus and minus sides of the second horizon, bringing the transformational paths into clearer focus.

A SHARED FUTURE CONSCIOUSNESS

Now that we have visited each horizon in some depth, it is apparent how natural they are – each is a familiar frame of mind. We all fit in with the practical first horizon patterns around us, have dreams for the third horizon future and have the sense of a good opportunity that characterises the second. We can also see how in the major activities of our lives we might be dominated by one of them: we might have an H1 position of responsibility running an essential service, or perhaps we have made a long-term, H3 commitment to pioneer a new approach to helping the vulnerable and are looking for people to back our vision and scale it up with H2 investments.

Of course, the infinite complexity of human life and change cannot be adequately described by the framework of a few lines on a piece of paper, but this simple notation of Three Horizons turns out to be surprisingly useful and powerful in bringing people together in transformative dialogue. It might be compared to musical notation, which is a simple way of representing the infinite variety of pitch, rhythm and musical structure so that music can be written down and widely shared. Before we had the musical stave it was very difficult to share music except by long periods of study and memorising with a teacher, and the composition of complex pieces for many players, like a symphony, was infeasible. With the five lines of a musical stave and some conventions, the explosion of creative invention that we enjoy today in our rich history of music became possible. Even improvised music that is never written down gains from the depth and breadth of musical culture that the notation of music provides. Similarly, Three Horizons is a notation that enables us to express and share the infinite possibilities of transformative innovation.

Although we can all adopt the frame of mind associated with each horizon, when we come together to explore the need for change and transformation it is easy for each of us to become stuck in seeing the world only in terms of 'our' horizon. We then talk with bewilderment and hostility because representatives of the other horizons don't 'get it'. With my H1 hat on I get impatient with the H3 pie-in-the-sky visionary and can't take the risk of committing to H2 innovation until it has proved its worth. Or, committed to my H3 vision that I just *know* is the future, I am frustrated with the obstinate refusal of the H1 dinosaurs either to get on board or get out of the way.

The essence of Three Horizons practice is to develop both an individual and a shared awareness of all three horizons, seeing them as perspectives that must all come into the discussion, and to work flexibly with the contribution that each one makes to the continuing processes of renewal on which we all depend. We step out of our individual mindsets into a shared space of creative possibility. We won't always agree, but we can significantly improve the processes by which we disagree, and sometimes even find fresh ways to get along together to support the transformations we all need – if no-one keeps the H1 lights on we won't be able to see where we are going. Just as musical notation allows a choir to come together and perform new work, so a shared practice of Three Horizons thinking allows us to convene a conversation of transformative innovation without having to invent a framework from scratch every time.

Future consciousness is the name we have given to this flexible awareness and skill that we can develop together because it is an awareness of the future potential of the present moment. This awareness is built on the three natural orientations we all have towards the future represented by the three horizons. It links these to a simple representation of change based on patterns, which brings a workable structure to complex issues. Through a shared step into this awareness we can improve the effectiveness of our transformative dialogues.

This book now develops the relationship between these three concepts of horizons, transformation and future consciousness around the following five propositions:

1. Future consciousness is an awareness of the future potential of the present moment.

This is the foundation – that we all have a natural capacity to relate to the future as qualities of the present moment, and that this awareness can be deepened through reflective practice.

2. Transformative change is that change which requires a re-patterning of our collective lives rather than an extension of the current pattern.

We are concerned with change at the level of the patterns of our collective lives, and how we work together to change those patterns when we decide that we need to.

3. Transformative innovation can be understood as working with three different qualities of the future in the present that we characterise as the three horizons of future consciousness.

The first proposition looks inward, to our own awareness; the second looks outward to the patterns in the world. This third proposition connects them so that they support each other: the three horizons are used both as objective descriptions of the patterns of our lives and as subjective qualities of the present moment. Working with Three Horizons to build a map of change therefore directly informs our capacity for transformational action.

4. Three Horizons provides a notation and framework for the collective practice of future consciousness for transformative innovation in a simple way – it brings all the perspectives and voices into the room with the potential for constructive dialogue.

If a pattern is to change, all those who are involved with it must at some point become engaged in the process of change – either supporting or resisting it. Three Horizons is a neutral notation for change; this neutrality allows us to explore what we mean by 'fit for purpose', and who 'we' are that are making those judgements. It reveals the perspectives of the three horizons in terms of both shared knowledge and shared experience, giving voice to each individual's view.

> 5. *Future consciousness can only be fully developed as a universal shared practice in which every person is a unique source of transformative insight and human potential.*

Our lives are a process of constant discovery and invention. Each of us lives a unique human life. Only by building a fully shared transformational capacity can the patterns of our lives give full expression to all our hopes.

The next part introduces foundational practices of future consciousness that inform Three Horizons work: seeing everything as patterns, putting ourselves in the picture, and convening the future. These are like the practices of rhythm, pitch and harmony that inform music, supported by the notation.

PART II:
THE PRACTICE OF FUTURE CONSCIOUSNESS

We all have some idea of practice as different from theory. Practice is something you learn to do, even if you don't understand *how* you do it. In the practical areas of our lives, like riding a bike, it is quite obvious that it is a practice, but when we are talking about ideas and concepts it is easy to confuse theory and practice, to confuse the sort of thoughts about how an issue might be tackled with the sort of thinking we are using to have such thoughts.

Over the last few decades we have become significantly more aware of the huge variety in styles of thinking that we use in different situations, from the routine to the creative, from focused puzzle-solving to artistic invention. We have begun to see that we can systematically practise different ways of thinking for ourselves and together.

Three Horizons has grown as a practice. The simple ideas it embodies for structuring complex issues have also turned out to support creative dialogue about transformational change. In writing this book I have attempted to step back and see what can be said about this emerging practice of transformational dialogue in order to help us develop it further. Three main themes have emerged: seeing, acting, and co-operating. First, by seeing the world as patterns constantly in motion we are able to locate ourselves within the processes of change. Second, from this, we can see how we are maintaining the first horizon or acting creatively to bring the third into existence. Finally, in a dialogue that holds all the horizon perspectives together, we can co-operate to find the paths for us all.

Seeing Everything as Patterns

Structure without life is dead. But life without structure is unseen. Pure life expresses itself within and through structure. Each moment is absolute, alive and significant.

John Cage, Lecture on Nothing

Holism with focus

Working with patterns of activity in the way we are doing here is also known as 'systems thinking' and there is a vast literature of many different approaches that has grown up over the last fifty years. Three Horizons can make use of any of those approaches, and is not intended to be a new addition to the collection, but a way of using them. The goal of this book is not to be a textbook or an academic review of all the ways we can think about human affairs as systems, but to orient the reader to a way of looking at the world that we all have and that we need practice to develop and use with skill. Here we are interested in that skill as it relates to future consciousness and transformative innovation, and we will focus on just the few main dimensions of pattern-based thinking that we need for that.

The best way to tune into patterns is to take a walk in the country and reflect on how you perceive and interact with your surroundings. First take a look at a tree. What you immediately see is its structure of trunk, branches, and leaves. What you cannot immediately perceive, but know to be the case, is that the tree is living and growing by drawing up water and nutrients from the ground, and capturing sunlight in its leaves to drive the process of photosynthesis. If you come back over the course of the year you can see the changes in the yearly cycle of leaf production and fall, and fruits and seeds being made for dispersal to produce the next generation. These and many other processes are what make the tree and keep it alive and growing from moment to moment. The structure of the tree configures the processes by which it lives, and those processes build and maintain the structures.

Our perception biases us towards seeing the structures, and only with the eye of our understanding do we see the processes. Once we tune into those processes we find we can keep working outwards from the tree, exploring wider and wider linkages with the rest of the Earth's ecosystem, and from there to its position in the solar system: from the fruits and seeds we can connect with the pollinating insects and the birds that carry away seeds and deposit them perhaps miles away; from the roots we can explore the many thousands of miles of fungal filaments that are part of the nutritional system connecting the tree to other trees and to the whole soil system; from the pattern of the seasons we can expand to the rhythms of the Earth's motion around the sun over the aeons.

Turning our attention to landscape and the weather, we can play with our ability to see structure and process. Our experience of the hill we climb is one of our own activity meeting the structure of the mountain, but as we see the clouds coming in we are very aware of the weather front we saw on the forecast and the rain processes that are in the offing. Looking at the hills we could equally well recall the TV programme we have seen showing the geological processes of the Earth unfolding over millions of years which shaped the hill in just the same way as the clouds are shaped by unfolding weather patterns. The more we get into the habit of holding both structure and process together in our minds, the easier it becomes to make the shift towards the processes at play which produced the world of the present moment and continue to carry it into the future.

Three Horizons thinking is based on consciously making this shift to bring processes into the foreground and explore how they

are shaping the structures of life around us, making a sort of figure-ground reversal in our awareness. Instead of seeing a world of stability to which change and uncertainty 'happen', we instead become aware that everything that seems fixed and stable is just part of a slow process of change, embedded in other processes that extend out as far as we want to explore.

We can naturally extend this way of looking at things into the way we see human activities at any level from a small organisation to the whole of humankind. Often a walk in the country will bring us to a ruined building, the remnant of a once thriving way of life, perhaps from a thousand years ago, or just a few decades. Contemplating the structure we can bring to mind the processes of life that sustained it in its immediate time and surroundings all the way out to the broader society in which it was embedded. We can also become aware of how those patterns gradually died out through the processes of societal renewal and transformation.

This way of thinking with patterns can be called 'holism with focus'. The focus is the topic of interest – the future of a community, country, business, technology, public service, or whatever. We develop a holistic, Three Horizons exploration by holding the focus in mind and becoming aware of all the processes that maintain it and keep it 'alive' in the broadest sense of a pattern that is constantly moving along, changing day by day in its first horizon identity. From there, we look at those ways in which it is failing to respond to emerging conditions and is becoming a less good fit for the future. We look for other places where new processes may be starting to grow as evidence of the second and third horizons. The fundamental perspective that drives this exploration is that nothing lasts forever – whatever is the familiar H1 context around our area of focus now, it will ultimately be overtaken by a new third horizon.

A good way to get a sense of the appropriate timescale is to think about how the current first horizon was once the third horizon. In this way we can see the scale of processes in play that gave us our current pattern, and become more sensitive to the

prevailing conditions and assumptions that sustain it and how they might change. We can see what aspects of the current pattern are intentionally maintained by H1 actors, and which are unintended consequences, outside anyone's direct concern. Indeed, many problems are precisely the consequence of their lying outside the intent of those who built the H1 patterns that now dominate: no-one, I think, set out to create an obesity crisis, but we have one as the effect of a complex interaction of many different aspects of our current way of life. It is this breadth of perspective which provides the holism – seeing the whole dynamic pattern of which our focus of concern is a part.

Patterns of renewal

As we explore our area of concern there are broadly two situations that are revealed by a Three Horizons analysis, distinguished by whether or not we have arranged society to support the process of renewal.

For example, in democracies we have invented a social system that generally is able to accommodate change without the need for collapse and renewal of the system of governance itself. In earlier times, and still in other parts of the world, we are familiar with societal change requiring civil war, revolution, collapse or some other discontinuous change in the institutions of governance themselves. Democracies do not work because we all agree on everything, but because the process of disagreement is structured and resolves itself in agreed ways. To champion change in a democracy you set out your manifesto and campaign for election. Your manifesto may include changes to the constitution that governs the democracy itself.

Another example is the way we manage our economic life. We have found out the hard way that planned economies don't work very well, partly because they are very poor at adapting to change. Their suppression of variety in the name of efficiency prevents the processes of change introducing and scaling up new things

through the messy competitive processes of innovation. Market economies are set up in ways that specifically support continuous change. Established H1 companies extend their familiar products and services as far as they can, sometimes absorbing H2 innovations, but over time most of them will be displaced by new players with accompanying waves of creative destruction across whole industries – most companies do not last more than fifty years as leaders in their industries, or even as independent companies at all.

Pockets of the future in the present

We rightly attach great importance to evidence in policy making – we want to know what works before we commit to it. However, when we are talking about the future, what counts as evidence? What evidence do we have for what will be invented in the future, or which manifestos will be written? Three Horizons deals with this by working with the three forms of intent we see in people's actions in the present as evidence of possible futures: whether they are maintaining the first horizon, or in some way acting to create the second and third.

By definition, H1 patterns are those that are well-established, that are maintained by our intentional involvement in them. That involvement may require us to exercise our intent in taking responsibility for them. For example, when a pension fund invests in a big company it is with the expectation that the management of the company will act with intent to deliver profits from the established business, and it constantly reviews the evidence of the management's ability to continue to deliver that intent over the years ahead. Many of the responsibilities of directors of public companies are established in law; if the directors do not act with integrity according to the expected intent to deliver returns to shareholders, they can face penalties. This is typical of the predictability and risks of H1. In every area of our lives, we place reliance on the intent of others to maintain the first horizon.

So, H1 evidence of the future is based on extrapolation – extending the current pattern of activity into the future and seeing what it will do if it goes on doing much the same thing as it is now. If you look at the stated plans and ambitions of any organisation you can get a good idea of what it is expecting to be able to do; it may be wrong, and you can make a judgement on that, but its declared intent is certainly evidence of its direction. Broadening our view, we can expect that many H1 patterns will persist beyond any particular organisation, and that is part of their strength; the intent to maintain the order of the H1 patterns is distributed over many actors in society and, when one fails, another takes over.

Evidence of the second and third horizons is found in the actions of those who are trying to bring about something that will challenge the course of the H1 pattern; again, it can be found just by looking at what people are saying about what they are trying to do. Setting out as an entrepreneur to create a new business, or as a reformer to change society, involves deliberate action, and a conscious intent to take the risk of standing apart from the extension of the first horizon. We call this evidence of emerging second and third horizons that we find in the actions of those attempting to bring them about, 'pockets of the future in the present'.

It is a familiar experience of futures work that once we have opened our minds to possible futures we quickly start seeing evidence of them that we had not attended to before; this is known as 'cognitive priming' – once we are primed to see something it can easily pop into our attention. There is so much information around us all the time that we cannot possibly pay attention to all of it, or think about where it might lead. Only once we have tuned in to a longer term perspective and primed ourselves to see the patterns in play does the small act acquire big significance as a harbinger of things to come. In my experience, once you have got some intuitions of what you think might be

radically new H3 innovations, a quick search of the Web throws up lots of hits of people already actively pursuing such ideas.

In summary, as a framework for transformative change, Three Horizons rests on a view of the world as constantly shifting patterns of activity providing the context for each other. We explore our topic of concern through the practice of holism with focus, bringing to the foreground of attention those processes that maintain the H1 patterns of relevance; we recognise evidence of the emerging possibilities of the second and third horizons in pockets of the future in the present.

PUTTING OURSELVES IN THE PICTURE

Only because we do not understand everything and because we cannot control the future is it possible to live and to be human.
Iona Heath, Michael Shea Memorial Lecture, 2012

Learning to love uncertainty

As an adult I had a chance to learn to ski – something I had only had limited opportunities to do as a child. As I rode up on the ski lift for my first lesson, feeling somewhat apprehensive, the instructor turned to me and said "My job is to teach people to love gravity." It was a startling introduction, but perfectly captured what I was to learn. When you stand at the top of a steep slope, nervously looking down, you are aware that gravity is definitely going to take you to the bottom, and the only question is whether you will do it in fine style or as a tumbling heap risking broken bones. You cannot ski at all on flat ground, and the skill he taught was how you must stand and balance and let gravity do its work, adapting yourself to the forces in play. He was right – when you get the hang of it you really do love it. And the more you love it, the deeper your skill becomes, and the more freedom you have.

All types of skill teach us the same deep truth: that the more we can immerse ourselves into the forces at play the more freedoms we have. We have all seen great players in sport when they are 'in the zone', or musicians giving a memorable performance, and been aware of how much time they seem to have, how they have a freedom of movement and expression that we can only dream of. In fact, studies show that the movements of a skilled performer are much more varied than those of the amateur. You might expect that skill meant more precisely

repeatable movements, and in a sense it does – in that it allows such performers to have confidence in what they can produce at any moment – but it also requires a deep and subtle responsiveness that adapts to the unfolding moment. Great musicians are never playing with metronomic constancy, they let each note live in the moment, adapting to the whole of their musical intent. The heart is the same; it is only an unhealthy heart that becomes overly regular in its rhythm, while a healthy one is constantly adapting the pulse in response to every signal in the body.

We don't have to be great performers or sports people to know about skill. Riding a bike and driving a car are everyday examples of how we develop new freedoms by transforming ourselves to engage more skilfully with the world. We progress from the clumsy stage when we must devote all our attention to staying upright or managing the controls, to proficiency which frees us up to think about our destination. Learning to read fluently takes many years, but the reward is that we can lose ourselves in the world of a story without thinking any longer about how we manage to make sense of words on a page.

The practice of future consciousness is also a skill, and the first step into working with the patterns of transformative change is to learn to love uncertainty. Change happens and, like getting down the slope on our skis, we will either respond in good style or find ourselves crashing to the ground as we meet it with insufficient skill. We need to become aware of the quality of uncertainty as it turns up in each of the three horizons so that we can respond flexibly with appropriate action in each one: we need quite different skills to compete in a downhill race from those we need to pioneer a new trail across virgin territory.

Uncertainty and change can make us anxious and fearful, and cause us to try to defend the certain and familiar. This can make matters worse. The moment you tense up on your skis to try and hold on and control your descent you find yourself struggling to maintain balance and a fall usually ensues. The longer an organisation tries to meet the transformational demands of new circumstances with more of the same that has worked in the past, the worse the final crash is likely to be. All organisations tend to be dominated by their H1 frame of mind which seeks to extend and protect the familiar patterns of H1. When the organisation is a good fit to its circumstances this is the proper and responsible behaviour that will keep things going along without disruption. However, when the H1 context is giving way to an emerging H3 reality, the H1 mindset becomes a barrier to transformation. Then, driven by routine and the need to protect what is working, the organisation can take on a life of its own as if it were a person fearful of change.

Perversely, in these circumstances, even 'good' managers can be trapped in the first horizon and lead their organisations to failure. This has been very well described by Clayton Christenson in his analysis of Disruptive Innovation, in which managers continue to keep their organisation performing well within the familiar first horizon context while failing to see that this is giving way to a new world – the persistence of many media companies in trying to stop the move to digital downloading rather than adapt to it is a present day example.

The experience of uncertainty is related to our H1 mindset which sees the unpredictable future as threat: it is the opposite of what we want, it is *un*-certainty. But the positive experience of the unknown is openness and opportunity, possibilities before us that we can meet with our creativity.

Within every organisation, the people who make it up are ordinary humans who bring their living H3 imaginations to work every day, and can naturally express their ideas for H3 change if given the chance. The skill of Three Horizons future consciousness is to make this natural H3 awareness a shared resource for change. IFF member Andrew Lyons recently suggested to an organisation struggling to change that rather than having a 'Bring your daughter to work' day they should have a 'Bring yourself to work' day.

If we are already pioneers of an H3 vision, living and working on the boundary of the new, we may already have a single-minded clarity of purpose and direction of travel. More typically, where people are using Three Horizons there is a deep sense of confusion about how to move from present crisis to some better future. In this case, the skill of working with the unknown is crucial, and can be thought of as tuning in to the forces at play and developing our natural capacity to work with them – learning to love gravity.

Creative integrity

We can call the practice by which we integrate the new into the renewal of the patterns of life *creative integrity – the making of wholeness*. To understand this properly we must reverse our habit of mind of seeing a world of stable things to which something mysterious called 'change' happens, and of seeing creativity as an occasional accomplishment. As we explored in the previous section, we need to do a figure-ground reversal to view the world as continuously producing newness, within which we create patterns of relative stability. Creative integrity is the process that all life constantly engages in to maintain its coherent identity – its integral wholeness – within the surrounding processes of collective life. It is the stability of the skier going down the slope adjusting balance moment by moment, of the whirlpool in the stream as water flows through it, or a life just staying alive.

When a novelist sits down to write a book, when someone we like agrees to go out with us, or we make plans to go on holiday, some parts of the outcome are well defined by familiar patterns of expectation – the publisher wants the manuscript promised by a certain date, we buy tickets for a show, and we make all the bookings for our holiday, but that is only half the story. The other half *is* the story. The story told by the writer, the developing relationship, the pleasures and disappointments of the holiday could not even in principle have been defined in advance, and nor would we expect or want them to be. If life were completely known and defined in advance there would be no point in living it, and in fact it could not be *lived* at all. We inhabit a universe that is always revealing new possibilities that have not been lived before, or old possibilities that have not been lived by us in our unique way before, and to be alive is to meet those possibilities in creative ways, renewing the familiar in our own way, and making our own part of the new together with others. In choosing how to be in each moment we express our creative integrity with respect to the potential of life – we renew the patterns in ways that only we can.

Each of us has to live a unique life and give it expression through the shared world that we enter. We each have to bring the possibilities and demands of being-for-ourselves together with those of being-with-others who are constantly experiencing their own dynamic choices. At any moment we can live and work within the established first horizon, or seek to bring about a change by standing out for the new in the second or third. We express our creative integrity in the choices we make every day towards the three horizons and whether our own sense of being human can be expressed through the familiar first horizon patterns of everyday life or demands that we assert the transformational possibilities of the third and accept the hazards of attempting to realise them with second horizon action.

In this sense each one of us is a poet, an artist, a maker – making our own life. Creativity is not the exclusive preserve of those people we think of as visionary leaders, artists or others whom we especially celebrate for their creativity, nor is it limited to the second and third horizon entrepreneurs and pioneers. The Three Horizons approach enables us to recognise where the patterns of our lives are enabling us all to live creatively and where they are failing to do so to the full extent possible. It is this failure that we experience as a losing of 'fitness for purpose' in the present pattern and as a need to move on. Then, indeed, the first horizon is experienced as a constraint on our human creativity

and the situation demands that we use that creativity to bring a new order into existence. We will need to come together with all those who have something to offer for the third horizon, and pool our creative purposes to bring it about. This will involve the skills of the settlers as well as the pioneers.

Patterns of integrity

Imagine being on a walk in unfamiliar country and coming to a deep gorge crossed by an old wooden bridge – will you go across it? Will you trust it? You have to decide whether the bridge is sound and can carry your weight. If it looks well made your concern is whether the wood might have rotted; you have to take a view on the integrity of the structure – is it still whole in the way you expect a bridge to be? If you come across such a bridge in a place where the paths are frequently used and generally well looked after, your trust in the integrity of the structure extends to the integrity of the processes that maintain it.

It is worth putting ourselves in our imagination in front of that bridge, pausing for a moment, and becoming conscious of how the type of judgement we make changes as we move between looking at the bridge and thinking about the people who might, or might not, have looked after it. As we examine the bridge there is a strong sense of objectivity about the process; we are collecting evidence of the sort that we call objective in the everyday sense of the word – something about the object that we can check. If we have companions then we will pool opinions and defer to expertise: "those marks underneath are a sign of rot – this thing is probably unsafe, and certainly hasn't been repaired for a long time". This process of judgement feels morally neutral, it is about the qualities and properties of a thing that is just what it is. In this sense we are examining the integrity of the structure as something independent of our behaviour towards it.

When we broaden our attention to those people whom we might have expected to look after the structure, we become aware

of a very different quality of judgement, thinking about the whole gamut of obligations, responsibilities, motivations, etc. that might be involved. This is very open-ended and uncertain. Are we on maintained footpaths in our own country, or far afield in unfamiliar lands where we don't know the status of country paths? Is this a place where there are high standards of integrity in public works, or is there a lot of corruption? This sort of thinking calls us to establish some sort of context for the imagined people responsible and think about how they might interpret their own relationship to that context. We are thinking about the existence or otherwise of some social processes, and the integrity with which they are maintained. This is a complex, morally loaded sort of process.

Thus the term 'integrity' holds together judgements about the qualities of things 'in themselves', and judgements about the human social processes that produce them; it opens out from things we rely on to how the actions of people relate to those things. The integrity of others is so important to us, and ours is to them, because it is the foundation of trust. Social life demands that we take for granted the integrity – the soundness – of so many things all the time, and the only basis for such reliance is that we trust the integrity of those responsible to put the preservation of that soundness above any personal demands.

This might be something as mundane as traffic regulations that allow us all to share the roads, or as deep and complex as the integrity we expect from our judges to uphold the rule of law within our sense of democracy. As I drive my car after its service I trust that the mechanic took the time to test the brakes even if he was in a hurry to get home; when I see the doctor I trust the advice to be appropriate for my needs even if he or she stands to gain from offering a certain treatment.

We identify corruption when someone breaches that trust and fails to maintain the integrity of a process that society should be able to rely on, and behaves according to some other motivation: an official taking a bribe to make a decision a certain way instead

of by due process, and so on. If a building falls down we investigate to find out if there was an engineering integrity failure, and then we enquire whether there was a human integrity failure such as a lax design process, or the use of sub-standard materials. It is a shock when such integrity fails or is lost; we are taken unawares. Much harm can be done, which is why we place such importance in the quality of personal integrity in those whom we must trust.

Going back to our walk in the country, we can imagine deciding that the only safe course would be to find a way to throw a tree across the gorge so that we could make our own secure judgement in its safety or, reluctantly, abandon the crossing as too risky. In these cases we are concluding that we lack confidence in the structure, cannot rely on the processes behind it, and must have recourse to structures and processes that we can take responsibility for ourselves. It is the nature of living shared lives that we are constantly required to make such judgements between relying on the integrity of others and taking things into our own hands. We can express this as a choice between the patterned integrity of the first horizon and the unpatterned possibilities of the third. We resolve this dilemma in the second horizon action that we choose, shoring up the first horizon option or committing to creating the new in the third.

An H1 pattern starts to lose fit with emerging conditions of life when people find that they can no longer fully express themselves within its patterned integrity, and must bring new H2 and H3 patterns into being. This can be for a wide variety of reasons: the sense of opportunity that drives a researcher, artist or entrepreneur; the values of a reformer seeking a more just society; or just a sense that the old ways are no longer working and we need to renew our institutions. This process of re-patterning, from the first to the third horizon, is the process of transformation – of creating a new pattern to replace the old. It is informed by our creative integrity – the power to bring new patterns of life into being. Exercising creative integrity is the only way to bring the second and third horizons into existence, because it is the way we realise the possibilities in the unknown future.

Creative integrity concerns our wholeness as humans from two perspectives: from our own perspective, what is proper to each unique life? And from the perspective of our shared life, what do we all regard as the measure of human solidarity in this situation? Creative integrity is never completely pre-defined, it is always essentially open in the face of the future. It is always 'unpatterned' because it rests on the unique people involved. It is the choice that remains when we have done all the due diligence, taken all the advice, ticked every box, considered all principles of wise counsel, and are still left with a question and a decision to be made: shall I take this path or that, work within established ways and means or pioneer the new? That decision belongs not to some abstract process that can be delivered to agreed standards but to a particular human or humans who, having taken it, will live out its consequences.

We have quite a strong intuitive sense of the two sorts of integrity that we have now identified that is reflected in our language of duty and rights. On the one hand, for patterned integrity we naturally speak of 'having a right to expect' that someone will have done such and such to deliver things we rely on to an appropriate standard, and talk of 'meeting the call of duty' in meeting high standards under demanding conditions. We are aware of how the expectations relate to the views of others on ourselves, our view of them in a particular context. On the other hand, for those situations where someone takes a stand in a creative and unique way, we talk of going beyond the call of duty, standing up for freedom, and so on, and we would say that we have no right to expect that of someone – it is an open ended situation in which each person makes up their own mind, and we might debate whether we think them right or wrong to do so. At the everyday level we all make such creative choices to live our lives in our own way. At the societal level we recognise that there

are existential risks that some are willing to take to assert human dignity that can only ever be freely chosen and never demanded.

Acting in time

The practice of Three Horizons thinking is always oriented towards action. It is a process of locating ourselves and our area of concern within broader patterns of life, and seeing what responsibility we can take for the transformations we desire. The exercise of our creative integrity in action is at the heart of what makes the three horizons three *qualities of experience* of the present moment. This is a central way in which working with Three Horizons is a common experience of the future that we can share across all our varied interests and personal contributions.

The first horizon is dominated by the quantitative sense of time as duration, a limited resource. It is the world most of us are all too familiar with every day. We have too much to do and not enough time to do it in; we have to prioritise tasks and allocate time carefully. It is the world of management, project timelines, deadlines and everything that involves the predictability of 'doing things on time'. The Greek term *chronos* characterises this experience of time.

By contrast, the third horizon is characterised by a qualitative awareness of time as a defining moment, a moment of decision. A decision does not have duration in time (though we might spend time pondering it); it is a choice with effects that will gradually be played out over time. When we take a turn in the road we have made a decision and will end up in a different place; it is the moment when a protestor decides to publish their views and take the consequences, or the policy maker stands up for a future beyond the established and conventional. When we hold a vision in mind it enters the present moment through decisions about which action will take us in the right direction. *Kairos* is the term for this experience of a moment that defines our future.

The feeling of the second horizon is opportunity, engagement and maybe excitement. It is also the sense of opportunity cost – that grasping this opportunity means giving up another, at least for now. This is the entrepreneurial feeling that comes with having committed to one way of moving ahead and working to make it successful. It is an experience of the H3 uncertainty and openness to the future, but with the flow of time meaning that this particular opportunity can be lost. We are taking a risk, there is the sense of *kairos* in the decision, and we experience the allocation of time as *chronos* in the daily work to be done. We are constantly reviewing whether to drop back into the familiar first horizon or continue to press forward into the third.

Whereas an H3 vision can be held indefinitely as an ideal and worked towards over a lifetime, the second horizon is a committed choice in the context of the moment, an attempt to capture the flow, to find the "tide in the affairs of men which, taken at the flood, leads on to fortune".

Convening the Future:
From Mindsets to Perspectives

Three Horizons is a tool for navigating towards our shared future and is oriented to action as much as analysis. A Three Horizons dialogue is more like a negotiation ending in a deal sealed by a handshake than a policy discussion ending in recommendations to be put to the executive. Recall the example of crossing a gorge, and the suspect bridge, and bring to mind the sort of discussion that would flow amongst a group of people faced with making a decision together. Some see risks, others are willing to take a chance; some will want to turn back, while others will come up with the idea of throwing a tree across, and so on. A decision has to be made, and how that decision is seen will have a big influence on the discussion. An afternoon ramble in the country is perhaps easy to abandon, whereas for an exploration of which this is just the first stage there is much more at stake.

In this example, everyone would probably at least already know whether they were on a ramble or an exploratory expedition, but in discussing transformational change it is often as if some people see a gorge where others see a sound bridge, and we don't even all agree what sort of journey we are on, if we are on one at all. Much misunderstanding will obviously arise in such conversations. A vision of how to cross a gorge you don't think is there will seem ridiculous, and if you are teetering on the edge looking for a creative solution for getting across you will be impatient with the complacency of your companion who sees no problem. I was walking some years ago with a group in the Lake District, and one member had a GPS mapping device, which was quite new at the time. We were coming to the top of a fell in the mist and our companion's GPS device was showing the peak as a quarter of a mile ahead, whereas we all quickly realised that in fact it was looming just yards ahead of us. Our first horizon maps can often feel just like that.

Three Horizons gains its power to inform transformational dialogue precisely to the extent that it enables us to engage our collective creative integrity to know where we are, to share our visions, and to choose the next steps of the journey. We don't have to know the future, we just have to find a path and avoid falling over the edge. We have to make decisions, and we have to make them standing where we are on the mountain. Creative integrity is not something you can 'do' for other people; entrepreneurial commitment, or standing up for a vision, are acts of individuals and groups who take such decisions for themselves. If we want to act wisely we will assemble all the evidence we can in a dispassionate way, but we will always be left with a decision on the next step, and it is commitment to action which brings about change.

The first horizon is there for a reason – it is the accumulated history of previous lives, and was once the third horizon of their endeavours. It has things to teach us as well as things that must now be left behind. The second and third horizons of innovation often involve shifts in power, with those who lead the first horizon giving way to new leaders of the third, or even more fundamental changes to the processes by which such issues are to be handled. Which future we end up in will have a great deal to do with how conflicts are resolved. The stories that are told about the future will always reflect the position of the story tellers, and which horizon is dominating their thinking.

Change involves gain and loss; there can be much at stake. We cannot discuss futures that really matter without working with our values and bringing into the room big words that are often left outside: hope, fear, love and power. The most challenging situations involve deep disputes about what we are trying to achieve, and who gets to decide: where one group sees an exciting opportunity, another will see a challenge to cherished beliefs; where some see in the current practices a

deeply unjust power system, others will feel threats to their identity in possible change; simple gain and loss of everyday personal resources and possibilities will frame the future for many.

In situations of deep conflict it is obvious that such questions of value are in play and must be dealt with, but in the context of our everyday organisational world it can seem inappropriate, impolite, to bring to the surface the really fundamental texture of change, which is all about how we are going to live our lives, what are our values, and how we will reach a shared view of the choices ahead of us. But if we fail to bring this language into use we are hiding the most important factors in the analysis and crippling the debate.

In IFF we have often heard people saying that they wish they could bring about a better debate between the different points of view on the future. We have found the Three Horizons framework useful because it naturally leads to an exploration of the values that underpin our current way of doing things and how these might have to change to enable transformation; it highlights how the horizons function as mindsets and how they view each other in the way the future is discussed.

It is the nature of a mindset not to recognise itself as such, and therefore to dismiss alternative points of view and to experience those as essentially 'wrong'. It is the step into awareness of all three horizons, and the ability to move flexibly between them that creates the conditions for transformational change which can pool the power of all three horizons to act. Recognition of each horizon as a perspective allows us to work with the positive aspects of all three and to explore what each might contribute to a creative response to present issues. This will not remove all conflict, since there will still be plenty of disputes on means and ends, but some unnecessary conflict is removed when confusions between horizons are reduced and we see that we might share deeper values in the third horizon than have been realised in the first.

Once different groups are able to see which horizon dominates their thinking they can also see how it relates to the others. For example, a passionate H3 advocate for renewable energy may easily forget what it feels like to have H1 responsibilities for keeping the lights on, and in return the H1 thinker, dominated by current concerns, can regard the H3 protagonist as simply irrelevant to their pressing needs. The H2 entrepreneur may be drawing their inspiration from the third horizon, but is also having to judge when the time is right to challenge the H1 organisations for dominance, or instead to work with them – whether to play an H2+ or H2- game.

The table on the next page gives an idea of the move from holding the three horizons individually as oppositional mindsets to a flexible use of them as perspectives that reveal their particular orientation to the future in the present.

Pick an area of your own concern and do the mental experiment of reading the table from different points of view typical either of one horizon (incumbent, innovator, visionary) or of a policy maker standing above them all. See how it helps you understand your own position better, and even if you 'belong' to one horizon see how you might open up new possibilities by moving to the positive column and engaging with the others.

There are no rules for who needs to be convened for a dialogue of transformative change but, by shifting to this inclusive view, representatives of all three horizons can discover more possibilities for acting with shared purpose than they had probably imagined. It is a natural consequence of a complex society in which processes of change are widely distributed that there is limited dialogue between the old and the new. We humans, being what we are, easily identify with our organisational setting, our most immediate tribe, and these loyalties can bind us to the mindset of the organisation. Given the chance, we can step out of that identification and explore the future possibilities creatively together.

H1

H1

H1 view of other H1s	H1 view of H2s	H1 view of H3s
NEGATIVE (MINDSET)	NEGATIVE (MINDSET)	NEGATIVE (MINDSET)
COMPETITOR	PARASITE of POTENTIAL INVESTMENT	FANCIFUL / Irrelevant what are they smoking?
BEAT or TAKE OVER	Watch and Monitor	IGNORE or KILL!
POSITIVE (PERSPECTIVE)	POSITIVE (PERSPECTIVE)	POSITIVE (PERSPECTIVE)
Useful Infrastructure. Potential allies for shared interests	Source of Abundant Ideas Change SCOPE of what can be DONE!	HOPE for the FUTURE Possibility of Renewal NOT CHALLENGING H1 ROLE: In fact, related to more of my life than H1!!

H2

H2

H2 view of H1s	H2 view of other H2s	H2 view of H3s
NEGATIVE (MINDSET)	NEGATIVE (MIND SET)	NEGATIVE (MINDSET)
SLOW MOVING DINOSAURS OBSTRUCTIVE (GET OUT OF THE WAY)	Competitors for Resources	IMPRACTICAL
POSITIVE (PERSPECTIVE)	POSITIVE (PERSPECTIVE)	POSITIVE (PERSPECTIVE)
• Destination for Innovation • Arena of Action and Support • Ways to scale UP	ALLIES IN CREATING MOMENTUM	Inspirational! Source of Ideas and Visibility SENSE of DIRECTION This way

H3

H3

H3 view of H1s	H3 view of H2s	H3 view of other H3s
NEGATIVE (MINDSET)	NEGATIVE (MINDSET)	NEGATIVE (MINDSET)
DIE: DAMN YOU and make some room!! LIABILITY OUT TO LUNCH	OBSTRUCTIVE COMPROMISE THEY are mis-using OUR vision	VISION COMPETITORS Debate aggressively
POSITIVE (PERSPECTIVE)	POSITIVE (PERSPECTIVE)	POSITIVE (PERSPECTIVE)
Potential Resource - when unlocked SKILLS TO REDEPLOY AT SCALE valuable Heritage + gains <<TO BE PROTECTED ? ?	Potential Allies STEPPING STONE PRACTICE SCOPE OF THE POSSIBLE IS CHANGED	EXTEND the DEBATE beyond the present brings DEEPER ISSUES of VALUE into play

Just as a sports team or a musical ensemble practise together to develop their collective skill, and in doing so enhance their personal potential as part of the whole, so we can develop our capacity for transformative change by seeing future consciousness as a collective practice and skill rather than purely individual. Through our shared understanding of the patterns and where 'we' are within them we can act with shared creativity and commitment, holding together as we navigate from the familiar to the new.

In the next part of the book we go on some Three Horizons journeys drawn from practical experience over recent years. They will illustrate some of the huge variety of situations where the common language of horizons is helping convene more fruitful dialogue and action than was there before.

PART III:
JOURNEYS IN THREE HORIZONS

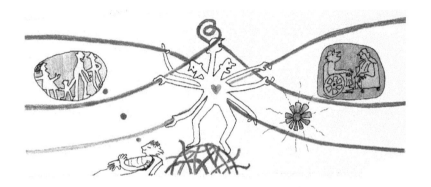

CASE STUDIES: INTRODUCTION

This part of the book brings the discussion down to earth with real life examples of the use of Three Horizons over the last few years. Nothing in the universe lasts for ever without change, even the universe itself, so Three Horizons thinking can in principle be used for investigating processes of change and transformation in any field. It is just a way of giving shape to our natural awareness of change, bringing it into our collective consciousness in a way that helps us act more skilfully together in the present moment towards our shared future.

Within the infinite variety of possibilities represented by the messiness of real life there are some common ways of using Three Horizons which build on its particular strengths. In any situation these will probably all turn up with varying degrees of importance and emphasis.

Sense-making

Probably the main reason that Three Horizons has taken off without any great effort on anyone's part is that, while being easy to understand and use, it helps people make sense of complex situations. The idea of the three horizons can be presented in a few moments, and experience shows that any group of people can then work with it to start exploring the issue at hand and make some useful progress within whatever time is available. From this easy entry much deeper understanding can be developed progressively, bringing other tools such as scenarios into use as appropriate. This is as true of a group of financial experts working on policy recommendations to government for hugely complex global issues, like the future of computer-based trading, as it is for a community group thinking about the local impacts of climate change.

Sense-making brings to the foreground our position as third party observers, looking at an issue to bring some understanding to bear on it, assembling all the facts as best we can. This is the outside-in stance, putting aside our own direct preferences and values except in so far as they are the incentive for the conversation.

There is particular value in the subtlety of understanding that comes from seeing that the three horizons are explored in terms of different types of evidence, and therefore different classes of actors. This allows us to explore the unknown and uncertain future in systematic ways. It also helps to clarify the distinction in the H2 space between those H2+ actions that develop options towards the third horizon and those H2- ones that might, or probably will, be captured to extend the first horizon.

Looking steadily and deeply into policy situations where we don't have answers is peculiarly difficult. Those groups that undertake futures work in situations calling for deep transformation often end up covering uncertainty and ignorance with over-confident statements such as 'this can be done if only we show the political will to take firm clear action'. Alternatively they put forward a vision or call for transformational dialogue to explore pathways towards a solution. The value of Three Horizons in such cases is that it allows us to hold a map of both what we do know and what we don't as a means of creating such exploratory strategic conversations.

Strategic conversation

While sense-making privileges our detached and analytic gaze, strategic conversation brings our own position and point of view fully into the picture. If we have come together to talk about an area of concern, then at some level we think that 'we' have a role in addressing it. Three Horizons supports strategic conversation because it invites us to bring ourselves fully into the room; we are able to recognise, make sense of, and think beyond our particular

horizon mindset, gaining a flexible consciousness of all three perspectives. In making this step together, all the voices in the room can be acknowledged and allowed to speak from their own perspective of concern – such as the need not to lose hard-won gains, for example, while having the courage to explore transformative change.

An experience that we have had again and again is that from the recognition of the validity of each perspective a more productive conversation naturally emerges. This is especially relevant where the issue at hand involves representatives of all three horizons in finding complex pathways that maintain the old ways while nurturing the new. While in some areas of society we are content to let emergent change happen, with the new ruthlessly challenging the old – in market competition for example – in others we find ourselves needing to bring all the parties together to ensure transition can be managed without too much disruption.

Public sector services have the problem of convening all three horizons of change to a high degree, because there are many imperatives for consistency of provision and maintenance of standards. This presents particular problems of introducing the third horizon in the presence of the first, to the extent that the first horizon can completely frustrate transformation however well-intentioned those responsible may be. Our example here is education where the need for renewal is clear, and where we are developing experience of Three Horizons supporting a strategic conversation that includes everyone from children in the classroom to policy makers in government.

Visionary action

From sense-making and strategic conversation we gradually deepen our understanding of the transformational possibilities of the third horizon and where our own journey lies, and who 'we' are that are going to undertake the exploration. Three Horizons

is helpful in the way it clarifies the context for visionary action by bringing into view the relationship with the other horizons. Assigning resources to H3 investigations and allowing exploratory projects to develop new measures of success can be challenging. It can require the H1 managers to go out on a limb to defend the new and untested in the presence of the overwhelming priorities of the first horizon. The power of Three Horizons to convene the conversation between all three perspectives enables the movement from opposition to informed collaborative action. This does not remove the need for leadership but allows it to be developed at the right level and in the right way.

The concept of the second horizon transition is very helpful in bringing the practical steps of transition into view. The Three Horizon map that is built by a team setting out on transformational change can identify which aspects of the first horizon will need to be carried forward into the third and which must be abandoned, and how this is to be accomplished. The distinction between H2+ innovation that helps create conditions for the third horizon and H2- innovation that will probably be captured by the first horizon is particularly useful for designing visionary action.

Patterns of renewal

As we've discussed several times, our societies have developed many ways to allow processes of innovation and renewal to go on: markets, scientific research, and democratic government are examples we have used. Three Horizons can be used not only within such processes by individual players looking to create change, but at the policy level of the process itself. This can be especially useful when those processes are not working well and innovation seems to be struggling to make headway. We can think of this as the 'Olympian view' of the horizons (in Greek mythology Mount Olympus was the home of the gods). The gods' eye view looks down on the three horizons and all the

players within them, and explores whether the second and third horizons have the supporting mechanisms they need to flourish. In developed Western economies an example of this from the last 50 years has been the systematic moves to encourage venture capital to finance H2, new business formation, and to create incubators and other supporting policies to encourage the exploitation of knowledge created in universities.

As governments look for fresh ways to bring innovation into the public sphere there seems to be a default policy assumption that it can only be done by market mechanisms. By using a Three Horizons framework it becomes possible to see that the market is not the only way, and certainly not necessarily the best, to foster the second and third horizons. Each of the examples below illustrates some aspect of how the project has informed the development of new ways to foster continuing renewal.

Voices and values

Throughout all the different uses, what comes through consistently is that Three Horizons awakens the future consciousness of the people participating and alerts them to the values at stake and their own individual voices. Exploring any situation in terms of transformation naturally reveals assumptions and values, and these are not just abstract notions; they are the ones held by those in the discussion, and those they interact with.

Case Studies

These six case studies have been written by Graham Leicester and Andrew Lyon of IFF and reflect the particular interests of IFF in transformative change. Three horizons is being used quite widely in the futures field, and some other published examples are given in the Notes to further illustrate the diversity of usage.

Carnegie Commission on Rural Community Development

The Carnegie UK Trust established a Commission in 2004 to look into the challenges facing rural communities and what could be done to address them. They did what Commissions of Inquiry do – examined evidence, went on visits and conducted periodic meetings to try to make sense of the wealth of information coming their way. They were also keen to take into account 'evidence from the future' and asked FF therefore to help them with some scenario planning.

IFF instead encouraged the Commission to devote one of its plenary sessions to an exploration of the future using the Three Horizons framework. In preparation we were able to scan a wealth of existing literature about the future for rural communities, including a recent set of scenarios for 2020 produced by The Countryside Agency and the results of an horizon scanning and backcasting project on rural futures produced by the Future Foundation for the UK Government Department for Environment, Food and Rural Affairs. We gleaned from this reading a number of important factors that might have a significant and unpredictable impact on rural communities, ranging from climate change and energy shortages to rising inequality and migration. These factors were then used to prompt a wide-ranging conversation that populated a full Three Horizons landscape.

> Sense making

In other words, the dialogue was able to respond to 'evidence from the future', but also place it in the context of the other kinds of evidence the Commission had been gathering –

> Strategic conversation

about the challenges facing rural communities (concerns in the first horizon), the promising projects and people they had encountered on their visits (initiatives in the second horizon), and the really inspiring work they had seen that gave them hope for the future (third horizon in the present).

What started to emerge in the Three Horizons session was a vision of the third horizon – a new pattern of viability and sustainability for rural communities in a changing world. This took the form initially of four different stories from four groups – but the common elements in them soon took shape as twelve key factors for viability. This pattern of twelve petals on a single flower became the organising motif for the rest of the Commission's work.

Opening up this H3 vision also allowed, at a subsequent plenary meeting of the Commission, an in-depth

> Visionary action

investigation of the transition zone between present conditions and the envisioned future. Most Commissions make recommendations for policy. This one made recommendations for action. And those actions were in part derived from grappling with the real dilemmas facing policy makers between continuing to meet the demands of the first horizon and moving the system towards the third. Working with four central dilemmas – for example between central service provision and local responsibility – the Commission was able to come up with its own agenda of initiatives to help resolve each dilemma, build on the inspirational aspects of present practice, and over time move the whole system towards a new pattern of viability.

The final report published in 2007 – *A Charter for Rural Communities* – used the twelve-petalled flower image on its front cover. Inside it provided a chapter on each 'petal' together with examples of promising practice and recommendations for new initiatives in that area. What started out as an H3 vision thus became a diagnostic template for existing communities to

Patterns of renewal

gain a better understanding of their own viability in the present, together with a set of resources to spur improvement. Significantly, one of the major outcomes from the report's publication was the establishment of a lively international community of practice – the 'Fiery Spirits' – dedicated to sharing their experience and their learning in trying to shift their own communities in the direction of the Commission's vision.

Transformative Innovation in Education

In the autumn of 2006 IFF was approached by a former education official and a headteacher. They had been involved for some time in a government-sponsored conversation about the future of education in Scotland which, with the adoption of a new policy framework called *Curriculum for Excellence,* had come to a close. They asked whether IFF could help them continue this future-focused strategic conversation since it seemed the world had not stopped changing, even though the policy was now agreed.

When introduced to the Three Horizons framework as a way of framing such a conversation, the headteacher immediately grasped its significance. "That explains a remark made by our lecturer on my first day in teacher training", he said. "He told us that he was training us to teach subversion. I never understood that until now. Clearly my authority as a headteacher derives from the first horizon. But my pupils are going to live in a very different world. I have to help them to discover how to live in the third horizon – in other words to subvert my first horizon authority. I must train subversives."

Thus encouraged, in early 2007 IFF convened an exploratory workshop to address the prospects for *Curriculum for Excellence* as a prompt for effective education reform. The event generated

a rich picture of the emerging policy landscape around the delivery of, and future prospects for, the new policy. Participants were also impressed by the way the Three Horizons framework had opened up the conversation and suggested that it might be valuable in other settings: teacher education, professional development activities, strategic thinking and planning in education authorities, individual schools, and so on.

Word spread and in time this activity began to attract the attention of Her Majesty's Inspectorate of Education. It too was interested in opening a dialogue about the future because, | **Strategic conversation** |
as one of the Chief Inspectors put it, the pace of change he and his colleagues observed in the classroom was just a fraction of the pace of change in the world. There had been steady incremental improvement in schools, but not enough to keep up with the world and so the gap continued to widen. He had therefore been tasked by his superiors to find a way to "bring the future into the conversation about school improvement".

He was also exercised by a second challenge. How, he asked, could the Inspectorate fulfil both its role of ensuring a good level of performance within the present system and at the same time stimulate the innovation needed for a very different future? Or, as he memorably put it, "how can we both inspect and inspire?".

He found that both of these challenges were naturally addressed when the conversation was framed in Three Horizons terms. It allowed the future into the dialogue, located pockets of the future in the present, and also naturally lent itself to an interpretation that was about both maintaining quality in the first horizon and also encouraging inspirational activity designed to enable the transition towards a very different future in the third.

So, together, IFF and the Schools Inspectorate collaborated on the design of a simple Kit that would enable school senior management teams to have wide-ranging Three Horizons conversations. Under the title 'Opening Up Transformative Innovation', the Kit is now available in every school in Scotland.

It is based around a set of cards designed to prompt a conversation about the present and the future. On the cards are a series of statements about the changing world, about changing education policy and practice and about changing young people (three suits). Every statement on the cards is evidence-based, about something already happening, at some scale, somewhere in the world – "schools become bigger and more detached from learners' local context", for example, or "a 24/7 technology-driven world brings an end to the school or college 'day'". This is a way of bringing current educational research and other knowledge into the process – getting the future into the conversation about school improvement.

The statements are then used to prompt a discussion (led by the headteacher, for example, with senior staff, around the staffroom table) that is recorded, on Post-it notes, on a Three Horizons chart (a more formal version of the chart shown in Part I), against the two axes of prevalence and time. Each card statement prompts at least two reflections to get the conversation going: is what is referred to on the card happening already or might it happen in the future? Is it a worrying sign of the existing system failing (H1) or a desirable feature for the future (H3)? The conversation flows from there.

With the addition of dice (to choose which 'suit' of cards to play), an egg timer to regulate play if necessary and a simple set of instructions to read and communicate to the other 'players', any group leader (typically the headteacher) can manage a strategic conversation that in a couple of hours (or less) helps the team to populate its own Three Horizons landscape.

At this point groups – and headteachers – typically ask how to interpret the | **Visionary action** | landscape they have discovered, and in particular how to incorporate the insights from their strategic conversation into a school improvement plan. Again working with the Inspectorate, testing and amending as we went, we developed a supplementary chart and a new set of instructions,

now incorporated in the Three Horizons Kit, to process the Three Horizons conversation and to draw out its implications for a programme of innovation.

This second phase encourages the group to identify and to embellish from their earlier conversation both a vision for the future and "hope and encouragement from the existing system" that suggests the vision can be achieved. In other words, they elaborate on the H3 ideal that they have identified and examples of it they know of in the present (anywhere in the world). Then they draw up an innovation portfolio consisting of three kinds of action:

- sustaining innovations required to address concerns about the existing system in order to keep it running (e.g. efficiency savings)
- aspects of the existing system that have no place in their imagined ideal future and therefore need to be gradually 'decommissioned'
- transformative innovation that will pave the way for their H3 vision.

The instructions also seek to remove some of the fear that surrounds actually embarking on transformative innovation by suggesting that such action does not need to be daunting. As the instructions say, the action should:

- Be small-scale
- Be inspiring to at least two or three members of staff willing to support one another in giving it a go (i.e. avoid 'solo climbers')
- Release resources from the H1 system and angle them towards the third horizon (i.e. does not require large, additional, up-front investment)
- Authentically illustrate the big picture developed in the earlier strategic conversation by fitting a transition pathway towards a vision of the third horizon rather than simply improving the present system

- Be viral in nature in that others will adopt it because it works and not because it is imposed in a top-down manner.

What these conversations in turn begin to reveal is a pent-up energy for radical innovation in most schools and always one or two individuals keen to try something different – to push the boundaries of their existing practice towards a desirable third horizon. But with no real management experience or support, no time, no money, no training budget, no consultants or facilitators available, how can these groups of teachers take the next step: the move from insight to action?

> **Patterns of renewal**

Bearing in mind the Inspectorate's desire to shift its own role away from monitoring towards supporting and inspiring change, IFF decided at this point to train a number of inspectors in a set of simple but powerful change management tools designed by our IFF colleague Jim Ewing. These tools dovetail beautifully with the Three Horizons framework. They provide groups with an understanding of the process of change, ways to communicate their plans to engage and enrol others, and a simple process for dealing with the worst fears of failure ahead of time in order to improve the initial design for an initiative and take some of the psychological risk out of it.

A year after first introducing these approaches into schools, local authorities and community learning settings, the Inspectorate evaluated the results. They suggest to the Inspectorate three broad outcomes in participating schools: a shift in mindset to believe that it is possible to implement radical change; a new capacity for leadership at all levels now that people can get a sense of where they want to go and how to get there; and an impact on confidence and skills for learning and for life amongst pupils themselves using these approaches.

Most impressive of all, the school pupils themselves are now taking to these tools with gusto. Three Horizons is being used in the classroom as a framework for understanding the dynamics of

change in all kinds of areas. With the security of the Three Horizons framework, staff are now happy to invite pupils in to open conversations about the future, and the pupils themselves report how the framework makes them feel like equal participants in the conversation – their voice and opinion valued like any other because it can find a place on the Three Horizons map. Pupils from one of the first schools to adopt the approach are now touring other schools in the area to pass on their new-found process skills to their peers. They also used the tools to manage a strategic conversation amongst all the teachers from the region at their annual conference. Transformative innovation is under way.

Winter Planning in NHS Fife

Every winter there is a bulge in demand for hospital services in the NHS as frail older people in particular fall ill, or just slip on an icy street, and are admitted to hospital. When their living circumstances are then examined in detail they are often found to be pretty fragile and it can take some time to assemble the necessary package of support to allow them to return home. So the hospital system absorbs the strain.

Because this happens every year, the government usually issues guidance to health authorities in the autumn with suggestions for how to get through the winter. They then ask those same authorities to convene in the spring to review their learning from the winter and pass on lessons that government can collate and convey to all authorities in the autumn in time for the next challenging period. It is a model system of continuous improvement… unless the lesson you learn in the spring is that you cannot go on like this, just managing to get through one winter after another, with the fabric of the system, already under constant strain, getting stretched so thin during these periods that it is at breaking point.

This was the feeling that prompted NHS Fife to come to IFF in the autumn of 2009 with a request to help them "challenge our thinking and give ourselves some longer term strategies for dealing with the limits to the capacity of our current health and social care system".

It was a clear request for some strategies for 'redesigning the plane whilst flying it'. They certainly could not let the existing system collapse – they needed to get through the next winter. But at the same time they knew that fire-fighting their way through each fresh crisis carried no hope for the long term. So they also wanted to be exploring new ideas for how to shift the whole system on to a more sustainable footing. Another image that came up in more gloomy moments in the discussions was of the liner and the lifeboats: we must keep the ship afloat as long as possible, but given that we know it is holed below the waterline we would be foolish not to start building lifeboats at the same time.

As a first step, a small group of local clinical leaders conducted a series of interviews with significant players across the system – the hospital manager, medical director, nursing director, general managers of the local community health partnerships, patient representatives and so on. The interviews were structured around the

| Sense making |

Three Horizons framework, without making it explicit at that stage. People were asked about their concerns about stresses on the present system (H1), what an ideal system might look like in which none of these stresses showed up any longer (H3), whether they knew of any examples where elements of that ideal system already existed (H3 in the present) and finally what innovations were already in train or planned that looked promising in their view as moving the system towards the ideal (H2+).

When the whole group got together for the day they were presented with the Three Horizons map of the landscape revealed by these interviews – a detailed picture of a failing first horizon system, an ideal vision of the characteristics of an H3 system, examples of present practice that displayed at least some of those characteristics and a raft of innovations that seemed to carry the potential to shift the system in the right direction.

The first thing that the participants noticed was that the third horizon they had collectively articulated was not very visionary. It looked more like an improved version of the present

Strategic conversation

than a real transformation. This is not surprising. The interviews had taken place with participants during the course of their working day, as they sat grappling with the challenges of the failing H1 system. In that context it had been difficult to come up with anything very inspired as a vision for how things might be different. In the context of the workshop, however, out of the office, away from the desk and their email, in a beautiful environment and in conversation with one another, the group was quickly able to stretch the H3 vision towards something with the qualities of hope and inspiration that usually characterise that space.

It was then possible to review both the 'third horizon in the present' examples and the examples of promising innovation in light of the new vision. Many fell by the wayside as being, on reflection, nothing more than marginal improvements in the present system – the kinds of innovation that had got the system through previous winters but were felt to be inadequate for the evident longer term trends.

Since the task from the outset had been to develop a dual strategy – redesigning the plane whilst flying it – the group then looked more closely at how best to implement a programme of reform whilst maintaining the current system. IFF talks about this dual role as providing hospice work to the dying culture and midwifery for the new. It was vividly illustrated in the workshop by the hospital manager who explained that it had seemed like a soul-destroying task to keep the hospital going over the next two years until his retirement when he knew in his heart of hearts that it was no longer fit for purpose and was bound to fail at some point after he was gone. But he was willing to keep the plane in the air now in the knowledge that it would provide the space for others younger and more energetic than himself to start designing the new system that would be fit for the future. So often these conversations paint the managers keeping the H1 systems going as dinosaurs, unwilling to change. In that moment the H1 manager was transformed from dinosaur to hero – keeping the forces of collapse at bay long enough for more hopeful actions to occur.

From this beginning – a single day workshop developing a new sense of the Three Horizons landscape – many new

Visionary action

initiatives sprang. Further analysis of the map allowed the team to develop a better understanding of the tensions that exist between the laudable values of the H1 system (efficiency, reliability, etc.) and those of the desired third horizon (loving, caring, human scale). Analysis of the pattern of innovations identified in the workshop offered six 'innovation pathways' to explore as ways of navigating these tensions on the way to a third horizon system, as follows:

- Invest in the third horizon as our strategic intent
- Evolve technology with a human face
- Grow the workforce to support and participate in the new system
- Engage in grown-up conversations – about living and dying, about love, care and compassion, about human limits and human potential
- Focus on person/patient experience as our most powerful learning tool
- Nurture community and relationships, recognising that most recovery from illness and longer-term care takes place at home.

Individuals stepped up to 'champion' each of these pathways, regularly meeting as a group to support each other and in recognition of the fact that all are inter-related. What has become most noticeable over time is the shift in the mindset informing the practice of the individuals involved, and the encouragement they have given to colleagues to participate in the same spirit.

The work has also generated specific new projects. The pathway relating to recovery and longer-term care taking place at home led directly to the development of a radically different approach to working with older people to help them live fulfilled lives even in their last years and to keep them out of hospital as long as possible. The promise was that in time this approach would allow the hospital to close an entire ward, with consequent recurrent cost savings.

The Health Foundation chose this initiative, the SHINE project, as one of a portfolio of projects across the NHS into which it put 'invest to save' funding. It is now in its third year of

> **Patterns of renewal**

operation. The H1 managers, in their increasingly desperate search for cost savings, decided to close a geriatric ward in any event soon after the project began, on the grounds that new approaches were now in place. One of the challenges for hopeful and inspirational projects is an H1 demand that they deliver at scale immediately. Those involved with the project on the ground continue to make steady progress towards their H3 vision by skilfully managing the demands (and the hopes) of the first horizon and emphasising the longer term nature of the transition of which their small projects are a part.

Even more remarkable was the link that the workshop and the Three Horizons dialogue forged with Southcentral Foundation in Alaska. Having articulated an H3 vision of a loving, compassionate, caring system, the group had looked for examples of this kind of activity in the present. One of the participants said that it reminded her of a presentation she had heard about the unique healthcare system developed by the native Alaskans. Further research revealed that Southcentral Foundation had indeed established a remarkable system of care based on the insight that health is a product of quality relationships.

This triggered the interest of the Scottish Government who also investigated the system further and, as a result, invited a group from Alaska to Scotland. This group visited Fife for two days: a visit from the third horizon! That helped to establish a link. Four people from Fife then went to Alaska to find out more about the system and to undertake their 'core concepts' training. The party included a local doctor in general practice who promptly started to adopt the principles in his own surgery on his return. Meanwhile in the US the Alaskan model was just beginning to attract attention, and in 2012 won the Baldrige Award for Performance Excellence. Remarkably, the tiny former mining village of Buckhaven in Fife was soon being mentioned in the *New York Times* as one of the places adopting the Alaskan way.

The relationship has gone from strength to strength, with a number of individuals in Scotland now having either been to Alaska or having studied the model. They have created an informal community of their own and are effectively pioneering together a new model of healthcare that in time they hope will spread across the entire country. In 2014 Katherine Gottlieb, the inspirational Chief Executive of Southcentral Foundation, will herself visit Scotland to encourage the effort and to share the lessons from their own experience in growing this new system, which itself started out as a small-scale transformative innovation.

Scottish Broadcasting Commission

In 2007 the Scottish Government established a Commission to explore options for the future of broadcasting in Scotland. This was and is a highly political issue, especially for a Scottish National Party government. The Chair of the Commission, Blair Jenkins, former head of news at the BBC, went on in 2013 to chair the Yes campaign for the referendum on independence.

The Commission, understandably, wished to take the future into account in its deliberations. Following the success of IFF's work with the Carnegie Commission on Rural Communities,

Sense making

we were invited to run a Three Horizons conversation with the Commission for this purpose. Preparatory research, including looking at recent scenario studies of broadcasting and civil society, led to the identification of a large number of significant factors that might impact the future of broadcasting in Scotland – including business models, technology development, changing patterns of audience behaviour and so on. We assembled around 80 of these factors on cards to prompt the Three Horizons conversation about the present and the future. We also took into account the three big themes that were already emerging as the critical issues in the Commission's inquiry to that point: economy, culture and democracy.

In a preliminary meeting with the Chair of the Commission and the secretariat we went through this pack of 'futures factors' and selected around 20 to be used as 'evidence points' in the Commission session itself. The Chair memorably called this 'selecting the hares we want to set running'. Naturally there was one card about Scottish independence.

In the session itself the Commission split into two groups, using the same card deck, in which each person was dealt a hand of cards and invited to 'play' whichever one they

Strategic conversation

thought would best provoke a conversation that they believed needed to be had. In this way the agenda was 'seeded' with the statements on the cards but in no way imposed: which cards came up, which hares actually got out to run, was down partly to the random process of dealing and partly to the judgement of the individuals involved.

The conversation was recorded using the Three Horizons framework and then the results from the two groups were brought together. After further work on the kinds of initiatives that might seed the transition towards the third horizon the group was able to create a narrative about the waning of the old system, the promise of the new and the critical initiatives and shifts in mindset that would support the transition from one to the other.

Participants were impressed by how much they managed to achieve in a day. The Chair in particular, who had been concerned about how to get the best out of the strong voices on the Commission and the diversity of firmly held opinion, was delighted by how the framework allowed each of their different perspectives to find its place in the story, and in the process weave a new story that none of them could have envisaged alone. He concluded that the rest of the work of the Commission would need to be dedicated to 'the transition zone' which would involve expressing 'difficult truths' about the unsustainability of the old model in a changing world.

The mood of the meeting was markedly upbeat as an inspiring and practical vision emerged, full of opportunity. As often

> Visionary action

occurs, it was possible to discern defining characteristics in each horizon which in turn suggest a direction of travel. In the Scottish story the shift was from a broadcasting system organised around government in the first horizon, through an H2 transition zone that privileged the individual and individual choice, to a third horizon configured around community. Thus in the third horizon 'Scotland' became less a geography or a political construct and rather an extensive community and a broadcasting 'brand' united around a set of common values.

One telling moment in the session was a discussion about one of the cards that simply read: 'New state of the art BBC studios at Pacific Quay'. This was a reference to the recent investment in BBC Scotland's shiny new digital headquarters in Glasgow. It prompted an interesting conversation about what kind of initiative this was – an investment in improving the first horizon or an innovation with an eye on a more distant third? How might this important development show up in the Three Horizons

story? "At the very height of their powers they opened a brand new state of the art studios on Pacific Quay, Glasgow. Yet at that very time digital abundance was replacing spectrum scarcity and public service broadcasting was being crowded out by commercial content as the industry shifted into a lower cost base, over-supply paradigm." It is doubtful that this would have been the perception at the start of the session. It is a classic example of Pierre Wack's description of really good futures thinking – 'the gentle art of re-perceiving the present'.

Southcentral Foundation, Alaska

It is possible to use the Three Horizons framework to understand stories of innovation and transformation which were not originally conceived in that way. As noted above, IFF has taken a close interest in the Southcentral Foundation healthcare system in Alaska. This is a remarkable system of care developed for and by the native peoples of Alaska, now attracting international attention for its results and cost-effectiveness. Viewing the story of the development of this radical innovation in healthcare through the lens of Three Horizons has offered some important insights.

First, it is a story that starts a long time ago. It has its origins in the conversations of the 1970s about indigenous rights and autonomy for native peoples. In retrospect those seem like the first moves in the story – 'H3 in the past'. They themselves were a response to the failings of a colonial system.

The H1 healthcare service that was made available to native Alaskans was condemned as 'second rate' at that time and so the native tribes began to come together to lobby for something better. This process of coming together itself can be seen as an extension of the earlier dialogues about indigenous rights. In a significant catalytic move (typical second horizon) the US Federal Government decided to offer the native Alaskans their own healthcare system, if they could guarantee that it would not cost any more than the existing services. That move triggered a lengthy period of visioning led by the Southcentral Foundation to design their own system – a vision that in practice drew on historic resources lying deep in the culture: the sense of injustice, and the idea of *nuka* (a native Alaskan word for the vast living system that sustains us all, the underlying cultural resources of recovery).

The visioning process thus revitalised an old dream now trying to realise itself in an unreceptive context. In the vision of the third horizon the flip has occurred: the dream becomes the dominant context and the alienation experienced in the existing culture is healed. Hence the guiding third horizon vision developed by Southcentral Foundation is of a compassionate nation, which in turn drives a strong, continuous H3 story of the recovery of values through a process of intentional design.

In practice, realising the dream of the H3 vision then involved lots of H2 moves – moves to disrupt and shift the context – to help foreground the dream over the dominant culture. The move from vision to action was initiated by a single dentist who made the bold step into the unknown, turning the blueprint from the visioning process into reality by declaring that he would put it into practice at least in his own life. He demonstrated to others that the vision could indeed become lived reality. That act of leadership in time encouraged a decision to turn over the whole primary care system to the new approach: as those involved at the time now put it – "doing that overnight was ugly!"

The next step in the story was to become entrepreneurial – to adopt the moves that allow activity in the second horizon to grow. Those involved moved from simply living their own lives in this radically different way to seeking to shift the context, recruiting and enrolling others, training people, running summer schools – developing an infrastructure for this new approach.

For a genuine transition to occur, at some point resources locked in to the H1 systems have to be released to feed the third. The Alaskans were very astute, therefore, in maintaining close relations between the H1 system and their H2 initiatives. They

have proved to be highly politically savvy, they have used high quality H1 performance measurement systems, they have managed tricky recruitment issues (from the first horizon) and have also maintained a number of shared H1/H2 resources (like the hospital). In this way they have enhanced the chances that ultimately the H1 systems will be able to follow them towards the third, rather than just writing them off as an anomaly.

This Three Horizons analysis of the Alaskan story provides valuable learning about the kinds of moves that the Alaskan system has made over twenty-five years to grow its credibility and capacity, moves that other visionary initiatives can learn from. The framework also starts to reveal – even to the casual observer – the kinds of moves that might come next. For example, given that the third horizon is always about moving towards abundance, it would seem that their next move must be to think about how to configure the abundance that their approach has created (rather than simply reconfiguring existing resources).

It also points to potentially radical moves in the arena of governance. It was a governance move that triggered the release of resources for a new approach: devolution from federal government. Then the Southcentral Foundation set up a board of governors. But what does the governance system look like in the third horizon? How is the flow of resources to be managed in the third horizon? They will need to answer those questions about governance if they are really going to be able to *establish* the shift into a stable third horizon. The Three Horizons framework thus starts to reveal 'the adjacent possible': the areas of inquiry where the project might develop even further, to answer the question 'what next?'.

The other revelation is the deep roots that often underpin stories of transformation. The story of the past should be part of the third horizon. What has been happening in Alaska is a process of internalisation of the vision for tribal rights within a context of healthcare. These are 40-year projects. We start from a current system that is no longer giving life, discover a vision for how life might be recovered, then all the other work is what has to happen to move from an externalised vision of what is possible to the lived reality of the changed situation. 40 years is a generation: from the courageous 20-year-olds who get started to the point where people are in their 50s and 60s and have the authority to make the transformative innovation the lingua franca of their era. The earlier decades are the 'preparation' – locating the dream, locating oneself in the dream and then engaging in the conversations to bring the dream from the imaginal to the cultural habits of the present. That process requires faith and persistence to sustain it. Viewed through the Three Horizons lens the Alaskan healthcare story is revealed as one of long term cultural renewal.

Climate change community action

IFF was in conversation in a Glasgow community with some people who had had a very troubled experience of trying to work together on climate change. These were very experienced, thoughtful community leaders of various sorts who had deep disagreements and were finding it very difficult to go forward. IFF did not use the Three Horizons framework explicitly, but used it as a way to facilitate and frame the conversation. What emerged with those people was that they were at different levels of consciousness in relation to the different horizons.

Some people in the room were very much driven by the external pressures of having a grant and being asked to deliver on that grant by an organisation that wanted outputs and outcomes to be delivered in a particular time frame. That requires a particular level of abstraction. So that was one level of consciousness. Others in the room were saying they understood that was what they had undertaken to deliver, but they were interested in exploring how that might be done without yielding the human dimensions of life in Glasgow, of themselves and others, that they were interested to improve; they believed that if they simply acted in the project in the abstract ways demanded by H1 they would not make those improvements; they would just be perpetuating the system that they thought was causing the problem. That was the second level of consciousness.

Then the third level of consciousness was expressed as "OK, so if that's the definition of the problem and the tension that we all feel and the fights that it causes among us, then how do we hold all of that and hold the idea that the individuals who are present in this situation must also be respected, treasured, maturely and in their difficulties, so that it becomes possible for us to get somewhere near our aspiration that people should live more fulfilled lives in this place that we love?".

Framing the conversation in terms of the different levels of consciousness was really helpful in supporting a good dialogue. In IFF we often find this in public institutions – people go into a mode where they have a particular language that is all about drivers and targets, and there's a whole tacit habit of thinking that's just present all the time and people snap back to it very quickly. Even when they are aware of a need to innovate and move on, the language tends to be about how to innovate within the existing paradigm, how to be more effective and efficient, for example. But, there is also a third level of conversation which is much more about the human dimensions of the system, which can be reached by framing the conversation with the three horizon perspectives.

Case Studies: Summary

These examples have illustrated in a practical way the five propositions that were introduced in Part I which tie together Three Horizons as a framework for working on transformative innovation with future consciousness as the practice.

Future consciousness is an awareness of the future potential of the present moment.

This is the foundation – that we all have a natural capacity to relate to the future as qualities of the present moment, and that this awareness can be deepened through reflective practice.

In our IFF experience so far, everyone can immediately grasp the idea of the Three Horizons in the present, and can use these three perspectives to open up complex situations to shared sense-making. These are natural perspectives that everyone has, and by bringing them into conscious awareness they become powerful tools of shared understanding and action.

Transformative change is that change which requires a re-patterning of our collective lives rather than an extension of the current pattern.

We are concerned with change at the level of the patterns of our collective lives and how we work together to change those patterns when we decide that we need to.

Three Horizons leads the conversation towards an understanding of change as transformation, from the pattern that is sustaining the status quo to a re-patterning that will establish the new third horizon.

Transformative innovation can be understood as working with three different qualities of the future in the present that we characterise as the three horizons of future consciousness.

The three horizons are used both as objective descriptions of the patterns of our lives and as subjective qualities of the present moment. Working with Three Horizons to build a map of change therefore directly informs our capacity for transformational action.

As the examples show, there is a natural flow from sense-making through strategic conversation to visionary action. As the map is built the team can see what needs to be carried forward from the first horizon and what must be abandoned, what is an H3 vision and what is a practical, entrepreneurial H2 step, and so on.

Three Horizons provides a notation and framework for the collective practice of future consciousness for transformative innovation in a simple way – it brings all the perspectives and voices into the room with the potential for constructive dialogue.

If a pattern is to change, all those who are involved with it must at some point become engaged in the process of change – either supporting or resisting it. Three Horizons is a neutral notation for change; this neutrality allows us to explore what we mean by 'fit for purpose', and who 'we' are that are making those judgements. It reveals the perspectives of the three horizons in terms of both shared knowledge and shared experience, giving voice to each individual's view.

This is the heart of the effectiveness of Three Horizons – that it changes the nature of the strategic dialogue, allowing all the voices to be heard, and shifting from horizon mindsets to flexible future consciousness. This means that the team can take a view on how to value the contribution of each horizon and recalibrate their personal relationship to each one.

Future consciousness can only be fully developed as a universal shared practice in which every person is a unique source of transformative insight and human potential.

Our lives are a process of constant discovery and invention. Each of us lives a unique human life. Only by building a fully shared transformational capacity can the patterns of our lives give full expression to all our hopes.

The movement to visionary action is embodied in the people who take part in the process. This means that each individual's unique capacities, values and visions are implicit in the path.

In summary, Three Horizons is simple to introduce, easy to use, and can help most groups make progress on complex issues. We are beginning to understand what makes it work. The final section of the book is a more speculative inquiry into these propositions to encourage further reflective practice, and in particular to develop a vision of the final proposition – what it might mean to think of future consciousness as a universal practice.

PUSHING OUT TO SEA

Writing is an attempt at some sort of truth. In Parts I-III I have tried to capture the empirical truth of the experience that my colleagues and I have had in our use of Three Horizons in a wide variety of practical situations. In doing so I was staying close to the shore.

In what follows I am pushing out to sea, trying to be true to what the book is about, that we each hold a three horizon vision which informs our life and which must be worked out moment by moment, constantly mixing with the currents of everyone else's life. I am trying to be true to the experience that I have had repeatedly over the last decade, facing what seem to be intractable problems and searching for ways to frame them that help people to keep working on them. In the most difficult situations I have looked for a way to steer across the open sea, searching for a destination that might not be there.

In the end I found I could only express what I was trying to do as "the patterning of hope", and I found in the story of navigating with imaginary islands, with which this book ends, my own emerging vision of how we might find our way forward together. These ideas come from the living edge of IFF practice and should be read as third horizon ideas, pointing towards a future only partially understood, and as an invitation to join the next stage of the journey on the open sea.

PART IV:

THE PATTERNING OF HOPE

KNOWING AND LIVING

In this final essay I am trying to make visible an intuition that is hovering on the very edge of my imagination. It is that we have within us a far deeper capacity for shared life than we are using, and that we are suffering from an attempt to *know* our way into the future instead of *live* our way. When you commit to making a moment of music or to a relationship with another person you speak to the future through that commitment. You bring the infinity of the possible within the range of your own creative potential. The way we have built our modern society has privileged the patterns of collective *knowing* over collective *living* and in doing so is overwhelming us with the impossibility of knowing what to do about it. By strengthening our inherent capacity for creative living we might find better ways to handle what we know and don't know.

I have found myself in many situations over the last few years where thoughtful well-informed people are wrestling with the intransigent complexity of our lives, whether it is the epidemic of mental health problems, or ecological crises and seemingly unstoppable processes that will make matters worse. I have seen the sense of existential crisis that is experienced when our systems of knowledge crush out creative integrity in health and education, and the way people in the arts must find ways to use first horizon measures to justify the exercise of their third horizon creativity. The usual processes involve assembling all the knowledge and asking how the problem is to be solved. Eventually, as the intractability of the problem is seen ever more clearly it becomes apparent that we are deeply ignorant: that we don't have an 'answer'. Then there is a call for a vision, for a coming together in a fresh way to explore how we might move ahead. Underlying this, but not articulated, is a confidence that hope can be renewed, that we can recover the human wherever we are. It is that

underlying quality that I am trying to frame here as the third horizon imagination in the present, a way of living into the future rather than knowing our way.

What can it mean to face the unknown together with skill? How do we rope up and climb a mountain that is not there? What might it be like if we regarded the third horizon as our home, rather than the first?

We have two sorts of knowing – one that moves away from ourselves and one that moves towards ourselves. Since the period known in the West as the Enlightenment we have had a particular regard for the knowledge we can gain by putting aside our personal perspective and finding ways to build knowledge together, especially what we call scientific knowledge. Such knowledge can be right or wrong, and is always being tested and renewed. The Enlightenment stood for the right of each person to be free from knowledge imposed by authority and placed the power of our individual and collective reason in its place. No person has any authority to declare something is right, only to say that it is as good an account as they can give of what they see to be going on and to submit it to testing by others. This gave us what we commonly think of as 'objective' knowledge – the testable knowledge of a world of objects.

But there was a cost to pay in this move. While individual reason, the right to think for ourselves, was valued, personal experience of life was relegated to being 'subjective' – which has come to mean arbitrary, mere opinion and standing in unbridgeable opposition to objective knowledge. The observer, the one who knows, the 'subject', was left out of this knowledge. All of this sort of knowledge is general, it can be tested by anyone – none is that which is particular to the person who lives a life. As a result, we find ourselves lost in a thicket of knowledge, where it seems that only more knowledge can help us, and more knowledge to work out which knowledge might be relevant, and so it goes on. Now we are opening up the great frontier of scientific understanding of our own brains and minds, and this is

exciting science, but still such science is silent on what it is like to stand where we are and face the questions posed by living a life: shall I take this path or that, commit to this act, this person, this possibility that only I can bring to fruition? As more and more knowledge is piled up, and as more and more demands are made that all relevant knowledge must be brought to bear on every action and every moment, we sink under the weight and find the ability to make simple human acts of judgement being squeezed out. In every field of working life I hear of people experiencing an existential crisis, an ever decreasing ability to bring their own sense of integrity to bear on the situation in the face of increasing demands.

The way of knowing that moves towards ourselves is the one that each of us uses as we go through the day sketching our lives on the blank page in front of us. As Viktor Frankl put it, after he had explored deeply the experience of those like him who came through the terrors of the camps in the Second World War, the meaning of life is not a question that we ask of life, but a question life asks of us. In this process we are not seeking to tell an objective truth that others can test, but to live a subjective truth – a truth of integrity told by the subject, myself, of this particular life that the universe brought into existence here and now and what truth it can reveal. The writer Ursula Le Guin responding to questions about the 'message' in her fictional writing, said that there was no message – the artist does not tell truth but makes it. A work of art may be judged good or bad art, but it can in no meaningful sense ever be called 'right' or 'wrong' art, in the way that a theorem can be right or wrong, correct or incorrect. Our lives are our own art, they are our sketches of our answers to the question of being human, and as such we and others may judge them good or bad, but not (in the sense I've given here) right or wrong.

If we are to release the full power of our collective third horizon imagination to transform our lives for the better, we must recover an understanding of subjective truth that does not stand in opposition to reasoned truth but underpins it, and gives it its worth in our lives. The beauty of the scientific gaze on the world is its deep humility towards being present with what is truly there, attuning ourselves so carefully to what is going on that deep patterns can reveal themselves. Good science is a work of love, uniting our own responsiveness to the full wonder of the world in front of us. A friend of mine, early in her scientific training, was being guided in using a powerful microscope to explore cellular structure and was told "You can only see it if you love it". At the same time, you must stand back, and as the great scientist Richard Feynman said, find every way that you might be wrong, explore every way you might have fooled yourself. Good living is more obviously a work of love, and needs the same deep humility and commitment to discovering what is humanly true, to revealing a potential for renewing and deepening shared life. It requires the same skilled, wise attunement to what is there, but this time to the truth of each human subject in the circumstances of the moment.

It will not do to put these two ways of knowing in opposition to each other and then call for balance; we already know which will win. Nor, as I discussed above, should we characterise our current age as being a first horizon dystopia to be followed by an idealistic third horizon utopia of universal love, always imagined but never reached. We need to understand that these two ways of knowing are in an important sense identical, that they both in their practice embody the creative freedom that is the natural mode of life, that neither is possible without the other, and that both require the courage to stand against inappropriate authority; in Václav Havel's powerful phrase, they are both ways of 'living in truth' in the present, not in an ideal future. Living in truth, without claiming to know the truth for others.

Imagine standing in the street with a map in hand. The map is a piece of shared knowledge like any other, no different in kind from the most profound theorems or the headline news, at least as far as this discussion goes. Experience of the world has been put in a form that we can pass around and use in a variety of places and times, for whatever purpose we like. It can be right or

wrong – a street might have been closed, or a new one built since it was made – but if we assume that it was done with honest intent, with all the integrity of map making, then what it represents is based on the original experience of the map maker. All knowledge is like a harvest from the fields, we had to grow it first; knowledge is just some experience that has been harvested and packaged up for later use. If we find a mistake in the map we might scribble the correction on it (if it's a paper one), or post a comment for others online. Knowledge trails life, it is the accumulated notes we've made on what has happened to us on the paths we've walked.

Maps can only be as good as the territory that has been visited, they are inherently limited to the experience of the world we've all had so far. If you live in familiar territory, that is fine. But we are all living at the edge of the map, journeying into fresh territory, and the rate of exploration is speeding up, with people heading off into virgin territories with barely time to draw sketch maps of what they are finding. Now, we might hope that the map making can get better, that we can capture and share everything faster and faster, and that seems to be where we are heading with our ability to link everyone to everyone else all the time; but that just overwhelms us even more. We must pause for a moment and realise the impossibility of the task. Nothing can, even in principle, tell us all the possibilities that stand just the other side of the present moment: what art will be made, what new discoveries will open up whole fields of further research, what new ways of living and being will someone reveal? However much knowledge we carry in our backpack we still face the radical unknown in the next step.

The unknown of our experience is not the same as the unknown of knowledge. Moving into the unknown and making it known in a new way is just what we living things do. A flower unfolds from the seed, becoming the unique and particular flower that it is in the interplay of its inner potential with the outer conditions. Musicians improvising are not lacking knowledge about what will come next, they just haven't played the next note yet. As the phrase takes shape it brings the next note into being. An artist facing a blank sheet of paper at some moment commits to a mark and the picture starts to grow. Each moment grows from the commitment of the preceding one to a particular path, a holding together of the whole with skilful care. Creativity of this sort is experienced as 'flow', in which inner and outer blend revealing the possibility that is here and now, and all who have experienced creativity of any sort know the feeling. Being in love is one of the most intense examples of finding deeper dimensions to what we are in the flow of relationship.

The idea of future consciousness is that we can link together our individual capacity for creative living into a shared capability for transformation. This requires that we hold our first horizon knowledge lightly, like a tune on which we will improvise together our steps in the third horizon.

STEPPING INTO FUTURE CONSCIOUSNESS

Transformational change is nothing new, but the need for a shared cultural practice of future consciousness is. We are at a stage in the history of our societies and the planet where people everywhere are looking for new ways to come together and change the existing order for the benefit of this and future generations. There are many people, as there have always been, who are leading thoughtful, committed and sometimes brave action in every sphere of life to change things for the better at the level of communities, business, societies and the world. Since the earliest times there have been leaders and prophets who can hold and communicate a vision that motivates people to follow them and rally to the need for a new order. So, just what is this proposition – that we need to develop our future consciousness – really saying? What will it add to the possibilities of trans-formational change?

The proposition is bigger than it might appear: while we have always had the ability to think and talk about particular visions, particular futures, we have lacked a shared way to think and talk about the future in general. We live with only a consciousness of the extended present, not a fully developed future consciousness. As individuals we have this natural capacity and great leaders have it more than the rest of us, but it lacks the depth and power that it could have if we made the step to a shared cultural practice. The way forward demands not just new ideas, a few more powerful concepts, but a deep transformation in the way that we *think together* to inform our actions.

Try to imagine if you can that you are an early human when language was just emerging. We can get ideas of what that was like from many other species – our primate cousins, dolphins, elephants – with their rich social lives and sophisticated forms of

communication that we are only just beginning to appreciate. In elephant herds the elder females hold the memory of the territory, and can navigate over great distances to find food and water when local resources run out. But the leader cannot (so far as we can tell) hold and communicate a vision of radical hope such as that of Plenty Coups, the Native American leader who brought his community through the destruction of their way of life when the buffalo herds were wiped out. That was possible only for humans who can communicate their dreams and hold a shared reality beyond that which governs their life in the present. Without language, at a time of crisis a leader like Plenty Coups would only have been able to lead like the elephant, setting off and calling to the others to follow, but unable to transform the shared way of life that might hold out the possibility of renewal and survival.

A step in consciousness is a bringing to the aware mind a quality that we already experience. In doing so we can give it form and expression such that it links together private experience into shared capability. This reflects back into our own experience, enriching, deepening and extending it, and the more it is shared, the richer it becomes. You cannot have a language on your own, it only becomes a language because the capability is developed in all – it is a quality of mutual life. You become a speaker by joining a community of speakers; even within the womb we are picking up the cadences of our mother's language, so that when born we know when we are within our own community, and can continue to grow into fluent membership. The step into language taken by humans was taken by us all and shows that there is no reason to suppose that we are at the end of our possibilities to transform our collective awareness of the world.

Looking at future consciousness in this way, we see that while we are all able to share and respond to visions of the future, and follow leaders whom we trust in movements of change, we lack the means to communicate and hold together paths of transformation through many of the complexities we find ourselves in – we are lost in the landscape, unable to map our

hopes in practical and effective ways. I propose that a shared future consciousness creates the possibility of holding transformational dialogue which informs our action in the complexity of the present while respecting the unknowability of the future. By regarding this as a form of consciousness we become aware of it as a *skilled cultural practice* like language, something that we have to learn to do together as an extension of our *shared* human culture that exists both through and beyond individual participation.

HOPE

We are exploring the practice of transformative change under conditions of uncertainty. But transformation of what, by whom, to what, and for what purpose?

Let us suppose that we approach these questions with an intent that through our actions we will deepen the life experience and fulfilment of ourselves and all the other ten billion or so humans who will be on this planet over the coming century, and beyond. We could approach the questions in other ways, and there is nothing in the practice of Three Horizons that requires that we hold this intent, but the thoughts that follow all flow from considering how we might develop our practice of future consciousness with that aim.

If that is our motivation, how do we act in the present towards the future? I believe we act with hope, with a belief that whatever the current circumstance there is a way to act that expresses the possibility of a renewal of the human. We act in such a way that our own sense of human integrity is given expression, regardless of everything that might attempt to deny it. If you read stories from those who have come through the worst that humans can do to each other you will find accounts of acts in which human solidarity is expressed and renewed in the face of all that would crush it. Or, as Havel describes in *The Power of the Powerless*, under an oppressive regime it may be an ordinary everyday act of human decency, just doing what needs to be done, that reveals the lie at the heart of the regime. Such acts may come with a cost, in the most extreme case perhaps the cost of a life, but they also resonate through the lives of others inspiring change.

Hope is different from an optimistic belief that things will turn out all right – they often will not. It is not a utopian belief that we can create a perfect society. To hope is to change our experience of the present moment into one of life, to renew the human where

we are, and as such is to experience life even in the presence of death of ourselves and others. Its opposite, despair, is to experience death even in the middle of life. The foundation of hope is the belief that in acting from our own sense of human integrity we are, in however small a way, creating the possibility of a wider pattern of human renewal around us. This may be on something as fundamental to our lives as when Malala Yousafzai insists on the right of girls to an education, or something that starts with the mundane, like a Scottish schoolgirl blogging pictures of her (not very good) school dinners.

We saw in earlier parts of this book how integrity, the making of something whole, is the concept that links our own actions to the patterning of our shared lives. Within the familiar ways of life in the first horizon our integrity is expressed within and through the established patterns: whether we are a politician or a plumber we turn up at work and get through the daily tasks meeting people's expectations as best we can, respecting the laws of the land and maybe making them. But when a situation arises that lies beyond the normal we may have no rules to guide us except our sense of human solidarity. Then we must make a decision, in a moment of *kairos* we must act, and act in such a way that we will be able to look back and say, given those circumstances we did what best reflected our sense of human integrity. Such an act may lie entirely within the first horizon possibilities, or may set us on a new H3 path where we become the voice and leader of change. It is when we must move beyond the moment, when the act turns into a task, that we move into the realm of transformational change as we are exploring it here – the purposeful re-patterning of our collective lives. It is thus that the third horizon is the patterning of hope through the exercise of our creative integrity, our ability to create new patterns of shared humanity.

It is not my intent to exchange utopian optimism for some other idealistic belief that we can replace the awkward, intransigent messiness of human life and conflict with a smooth

and harmonious process of universal agreement on our vision of the future. What I want to suggest is that the step into future consciousness will enable us to strengthen our ability to work with our moral imaginations to forge new paths together.

As we explored earlier, once we start to investigate the third horizon of our topic of concern we are faced with the question of what counts as evidence. We saw how the intent of others is one sort of evidence: if people do what they say they are trying to do, we can get an idea of what sort of future they will create. If we imagine bringing all those people into one room then the uncertainty of the future has become a discussion, a debate, or a dialogue between competing views and positions; our uncertainty about the future has become the real life drama of our politics.

It does not take much experience of life to know that we can never establish an agreed starting point for any discussion when politics and deep values are at stake. It only takes one person to say "at least we can agree for a start that..." for someone else to disagree, and so it goes. However, as we saw in Part II, human society has gradually developed ways to disagree productively, so that our first horizon life is the outcome of agreed H2 and H3 processes of change.

Democracy turns the need for revolutionary change into one of orderly replacement of government; and it has special mechanisms for constitutional change of the replacement/ renewal process itself. The scientific process that underpins our technological society had to be invented over several centuries, and rests on the careful organisation of continuous peer review that enables individual views of the world to be tested, rejected, improved and accepted. Market economies rely on the new challenging the old within a well-understood regime of organisational life, with separate institutions for new ventures in the second horizon, and exploratory research in the third.

In these and other areas of our lives the positive result of these processes is that we can greatly deepen the cultural learning that is carried on through the cycles of renewal: we extend and

improve our range of democratic institutions; we constantly expand our scientific knowledge of the world; we enjoy the fruits of the extraordinary variety of innovation that our modern economies produce. We can carry forward what is useful from the old while bringing in the new.

The idea of future consciousness can be seen as a further step to improve the ways we work with individual creativity in order to strengthen our shared lives, a step that is necessary to support the cultural innovation we need for the circumstances we find ourselves in.

TRANSFORMATIVE SOCIETY

Society (n): an instance of association or companionship with others.

Oxford English Dictionary

We started our enquiry into the practice of future consciousness with the idea of skill, and how skill gives us freedoms. To the extent that we can attune our own capabilities to those of the world in which we live, we can work skilfully to create possibilities for ourselves and others. If we don't encounter the world skilfully then we will suffer change and be subject to it – gravity will take us down the mountain one way or another.

We have built ourselves a world in which change is happening at greater speed and with greater scope and interdependence than ever before, and where those processes are feeding on themselves to further increase the speed and scope of change. We humans have great transformative potential to renew the qualities of human life under new conditions, but just now many of us are getting overwhelmed and suffering. We live in a paradox: we must each assemble all the dimensions of a culture for ourselves within the bewildering variety of choices available that change from day to day, and yet culture is inherently shared, and everyone else is busy trying to assemble their own pattern of life. We need to find a way to make our home together in these changing patterns by sharing our transformative potential, so that each of us is participating in the flow of skilled living with each other, rather than being battered about and landing with broken bones or spirit.

A group of musicians improvising together has to work with the same paradox. Once a theme is chosen then only by responding to each other can they fulfil a common purpose –

such unity cannot be given in advance, it can only be made in the moment and, in the making, it enhances the freedoms from which it is made. In this sense you become a musician by joining a community of musicians, developing your skilled freedoms in concert with others. Imagine such a group where one of the players comes up with a little phrase he likes and then hangs on to playing it over and over, holding back the whole flow. It just can't work unless everyone moves together. The creative integrity of the ensemble flows together or it doesn't flow at all. The whole emerges from the constant interplay of moving parts, creating new possibilities for each one. The skill of one player can lift that of others. If we're lucky we have experienced for ourselves how our own performance is raised to a new level by participating with a skilled practitioner.

Some practices are minority interests and are pursued by those who care about them, without much concern for, or interest from, the rest of society – in most countries it really doesn't matter how many people learn to ski. However, there are some practices that are carried forward best at the level of society as a whole. Democracy is a defining example. The whole point of democracy is that it is built on the involvement of everyone. Whether or not we use our vote, we all expect to participate in the give and take of argument on the direction of society and to use our freedom of speech and association to influence the flow of public opinion when it matters to us. In this case, practice at an individual level is essential to support the practice in the large, and our politics is weakened overall if any individual is disenfranchised. Language, literacy and numeracy are another case. They are so important for the individual and for society as a whole that we devote great resources to ensuring we cultivate them in every generation; our society is weakened overall if any individual does not share these basic capacities.

We talk, appropriately, of building a democratic society, a literate society and so on, characterising a whole society by the universal practice of these qualities. Likewise, I suggest we might

talk of a transformative society as one that has cultivated the universal practice of future consciousness.

By practising future consciousness together we create possibilities of skilled creative living under conditions of change that are inaccessible while we practise alone. If one of us holds on to our favourite first horizon phrase, the rest cannot play their own third horizon music – in the worst case we just have a cacophony of parts, tentative and uncertain starts at new phrases, but no collective music, each note dying out in the general confusion.

Future consciousness changes our awareness and our relationship with each other. To recognise that continuous transformation is the process of our creative lives together, we need to see each person as the holder of a unique insight into the emerging third horizon. By developing such a view we grant the power of fulfilment to each other. I believe that only an ambition to create a shared future consciousness for every human being, one that recognises the unique qualities of hope that each person embodies, can create a society which realises the potential of us all.

This ambition raises the question of what sorts of organisations might foster this practice. Democracy and literacy are maintained by a wide range of social institutions. The freedoms of the market rely on agreements at every level from the local to the global. What direction might we take to develop future consciousness not just individually but at the level of our organisational life?

I want to contrast two kinds of organisation according to where their main effect is produced: on the outside or the inside. First there are businesses and social enterprises that produce results on the outside. A business exists to make a living for those involved, and a profit for its owners (if those two classes of people are different). Social enterprises and charities exist to achieve some effect in the world beyond themselves, and raise money which they channel to this purpose.

Then there are the organisations in which people come together to pursue a common interest: clubs and societies in which people play football, read books, paint, or whatever. The main feature of such organisations is that they do not exist for a purpose beyond themselves and they use resources just to pursue their interests. Of course they do have effects in the wider society, but these are secondary, and any fundraising efforts are a side-effect of the primary purpose. The results are on the inside, in the game played, the conversation enjoyed, the picture painted, and the fellowship of the social life that goes on in the doing. In many cases the activity is just the means of creating the opportunity for such fellowship among friends.

I will call these sorts of organisations simply 'societies'. In doing so I intend there to be the resonance and ambiguity with broader society, the setting within which we all live our lives at multiple scales from the family to the whole of humankind: we all belong to the society of the human life we have in common.

Just as businesses may have goals that might be judged by others as good or bad for our common life, so it is important to recognise there is nothing in this notion of society that means that a particular instance of a society is intrinsically 'good' from any perspective other than that of its members. A bizarre cult that indoctrinates its members in destructive beliefs and closes itself to outside influence is as much a society as any that commands widespread support, such as democratic society for example.

Organisations that have their results on the outside commonly think of themselves as 'adding' value *in* the product or service they offer to the world. They use resources internally to make their product or service, and this then enables the rest of us to do something we want to do that we could not do so easily otherwise – value has been produced *by* the organisation. This way of thinking fits very naturally with the industrial era of the last couple of hundred years in which we have seen the extraordinary expansion of 'stuff' that we can invent and manufacture for every possible use.

However, as is well known by economists, you can never actually pin down what this 'value' is that is supposedly 'in' the stuff, because in fact the value arises in the use, and those uses happen within a particular life, in particular and unique ways, and there is no general measure of these qualities of interaction. When you drive your car, use your iPod, look at a Picasso or eat a banana, *you* make the value in the moment of interaction. The car, the iPod, the picture and the fruit enable the value creation, but the value itself is a quality of life for the one who experiences it: the utility of getting from A to B, and perhaps the status of owning a fine car; the pleasure of listening to the music or enjoying the picture, and the wider interest you have in music or art; the quick snack that keeps you going, or an ingredient in a meal you make for others. Value in this sense is made in the life and lives in which the thing is taken up and takes part; value is *for a life in a pattern of relationships.*

I find that most discussions of policy and the problems of society-at-large are cast in terms of the contrast between the two sorts of organisation that have results on the outside – between profits and non-profits, business and the public sector – with societies being left out of the picture. I suggest that in doing so we are failing to see that, in the end, all the value of society is on the inside – in the ways we fulfil our individual lives in the richness of mutual life in all its forms. It is in strengthening such patterns and the organisational forms that support them that we find the direction for transformative innovation which leads to a deeper fulfilment for everyone.

I see in societies the natural organisation of shared practice, embodying particular qualities of life 'on the inside'. Perhaps if we can expand this way of living together, we can counteract some of the effects of the other ways of organising that have such powerful unintended effects outside themselves but within our society at large.

Navigating on the Open Sea

Conscious change calls for a recognition of consciousness and calls for the inner work to develop wholeness in the moment.

Karen O'Brien

Since this book was first published the sense that we face existential threats from climate change and the pressures on the Earth's natural systems has grown and is now widespread. Many people are looking for ways to answer the urgent questions: how are we to ensure that ten billion people or more will be able to thrive together on one planet? How can we find new ways of living together that will restore a positive relationship between human civilisation and our living planetary home?

A change in worldview is needed, a clearer understanding of our place within the landscape, so that we can act to restore and maintain the relationships that make us and the Earth a living whole. In this final part I would like to draw together the ideas in the book and offer a simple guide to developing the future consciousness with which we can learn together with our whole person in the whole human and planetary system in which we live.

The foundational awareness we need to develop is *holism with focus* – to see the world in patterns and to recognise our own role in how those patterns are carried forward. A simple but powerful way to awaken this dual awareness in our minds is shown on the next page, with the words making a continuous sentence: *the pattern connects the lives that embody...*

Each act we take, in every moment, is part of an existing pattern, or starts to create a new one, and the pattern gives meaning to the acts and is carried forward by them. We are directly and immediately aware of our actions; this is the mental

focus of the moment. At the same time the actions are always related to the contextual pattern that gives them meaning, but awareness of the pattern generally lies just below the surface of our consciousness, unless there is some reason to bring it to mind. This is the holism we need to develop.

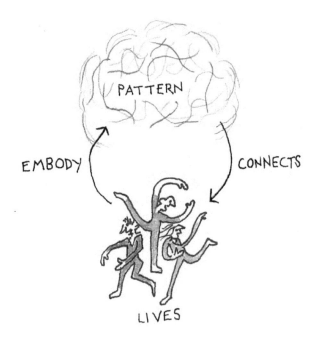

Recall for a moment how you have gone through your day, carrying out tasks that connect any one moment to a longer and wider pattern. Reflect how each act gained its meaning from its context, and how automatic that was most of the time. It might be as simple as singing a tune in which each note makes up the melody, joining the flow of commuters, arriving at the office and dropping into the usual routine, or a moment of thoughtful reflection such as standing in the polling booth hesitating before placing your cross on the paper. The pattern is not something other than the acts of participation that make it up any more than the melody is different from the notes. As the poet

Machado put it: 'the path is made by walking'. All we need to do is to practise bringing the path into view as well as the steps, not only the single notes but the whole melody of life into our conscious awareness.

As you work with Three Horizons keep this picture in view – of patterns connecting lives that in turn embody patterns – and it will help you deepen your understanding of future consciousness and put it into practice. It opens up the pattern dimension of our lives that is behind and within each moment, often as an unexamined habit of heart and mind.

Setting out to sea

One of my favourite metaphors for future consciousness comes from the Polynesian sailors who navigate with the help of imagined islands. In order to reach distant specks of land across the open seas they make use of many clues from the sun and tides, as well as using all the islands along the way to get their bearings. But they also structure their journey with the help of imagined islands which provide mental images that help them with the complex task of finding their way. These are not visions of the destination, nor are they pathways, but they offer an image to help hold all the subtle indicators together in the minds of the sailors such that the true way may be found. The placing and pattern of these islands and their relationship to observable phenomena is a shared cultural form passed across the generations.

In that spirit, what follows is a reflection on those imaginary islands that we might hold as qualities of future consciousness to help us to find our way into a flourishing future for people and planet. Each of them encourages us to think in terms of wider patterns and our own and others' participation in them. I can offer four.

The island of Abundance

Life creates conditions conducive to life.

Janine Benyus

The first island is one of paradox, of the seeming impossibility of life arising on a lifeless land and sea beaten by the sun.

Contemplate the history of the planet Earth; imagine looking at it before there was any life on it and trying to envisage what sort of processes could cover it with the abundance of life we see, powered only by the sun falling on the empty seas and bare rock. Imagine too trying to anticipate that over the millennia life would not only increase in scale and complexity, but would deposit huge quantities of concentrated energy in the ground; imagine life lived to such a level of abundant intensity that riches are left behind.

Life arises as a configuration of flows of energy, giving it form and structure. While any one life may have to experience competition for resources, and scarcity, and all must eventually die, overall life itself is a manifestation of flow and abundance.

As we have used up the stored riches we inherited on Earth, it seems that our future must be one of scarcity, but life must always be a configuration of abundance, and it is only toward this sense of the potential of life that we can navigate with hope. This need not be a blind hope that we can go on with our H1 patterns exhausting themselves using up historic stocks; rather it is to see that life takes what is there and realises itself in creative flows.

In many foresight discussions I have seen how the assumption of our traditional economic thinking that value derives from scarcity freezes the third horizon imagination. Simply inviting people to look for sources of abundance releases creative potential. Like the sun on the bare sea and rock, these sources might seem paradoxical at first. A deprived community has an abundance of human hope and potential looking for an outlet in a barren environment. The first step into the third horizon is to see all that is there with the eye of creative potential. It is to see what is there, already in abundance, that can come together in new life-creating patterns of society.

The island of Infinite Variety

Look at a rain forest and reflect on the enormous diversity of species that are there. Life is plural, made up from the interaction of diverse forms, each creating the conditions of life for the others. The abundance of life is an abundant variety, where the depth and intensity of interaction drives more growth and diversity.

The dynamic of life is a constant interplay between the particular and the general, the individual life and the community of lives. To be a living thing is to have a perspective on the world, to be in relationship with that world. Some things are food, some are poison, some are mates, some are predators, and so on. Each life brings forth a world in a unique way, but can only do so in relationship to others. Each life contributes its uniqueness to the patterns of which it is a part. Transformational change comes about, as when a caterpillar turns into a butterfly, by reconfiguring those relationships of identity and viability that connect the particular life to the whole.

Looking more deeply into the history of the planet we see that the abundance that we have lived off is itself a consequence of major transitions in the mutually maintained complexity of patterns of life: from anaerobic forms that flooded the atmosphere with oxygen to aerobic life; from the simplest life forms to the complex cells that embedded the simpler forms for energy; from single cells to the multi-cellular transition that enabled the Cambrian explosion; from plants to animals.

All evolution is co-evolution, and each major transition has expanded the basic patterns of life from which a new scale of complexity can emerge.

In our human history, our critical transition has been the one to the industrial economy which led to a rapid expansion in the scale and complexity of ways of making a living. It is this that has brought us our problematic prosperity. Over these brief three centuries we have changed the planet: just like the cyanobacteria that filled the atmosphere with toxic oxygen and set the scene for the emergence of aerobic life, we have rapidly changed the eco-sphere so that a transition is inevitable.

We might gain metaphorical inspiration from the way the complex cells that made the Cambrian explosion possible absorbed the simpler bacteria as energy sources. It seems that the energy demands of the cells that make up all the familiar plants and animals around us can only be met by hosting within them the simpler sorts of life. Similarly, when I see creative people and organisations using a whole variety of different sorts of business organisation to fulfil their creative passion, I like to think that they are pioneering this fundamental transition. They are interested in turning money into meaning, rather than meaning into money, and use business structures embedded within them to do so.

I suggest that we renew our understanding of society, recognising it as the organisational form that sustains the abundance of unique qualities of life within itself. There is no 'outside' on this shared planet, and we must adopt ways of thinking that see value, health and wealth where they are – within the patterns of mutually sustaining organisation. There is no obvious limit to our potential to bring new forms of shared life into existence that enrich the possibilities of life's flow.

The island of Mutuality

How many songs can be sung, how many things can be said, how many books can be written?

Place yourself, if you can, in a world of people without songs, words or books, and imagine how you could have given meaning to the idea of a spoken and written language and its potential to expand infinitely the possibilities of shared life. Language, like life, is a mutual property: language extends and deepens the mutuality of life; it belongs to no one life completely but is carried forward by all of them; it brings forth new worlds of self-sustaining diversity.

It is quite hard to get hold of the idea of a mutual quality of life as I want to express it – the notion that there are capabilities we have that we cannot have alone, that are brought forth only in patterns of relationship. A way to illustrate it is with a fascinating little experiment you can do with a couple of spoons and three pieces of string. Hang each of the spoons from a piece of string that is tied like a washing line between two chairs. Set the first spoon swinging while the other hangs still. As the first spoon swings, little by little the second one starts to swing also, but not in time with the first, picking up more and more energy until it is the one swinging and the first one comes almost to rest. Then the process reverses, and the first one picks up again while the second one comes to rest. And so on, and on. Add more spoons and the patterns become even more varied and fascinating.

Each spoon produces a behaviour that is quite different from what it would produce on its own, and the cause cannot be found in anything less than the complete configuration of spoons and string. This is a simple demonstration of mutual co-ordination, in which things link together to create emergent patterns that change what each of the participants can do. If we zoom in and

look at one spoon hanging there and try to understand its behaviour without seeing the other one and how they are coupled, we will never work out what is going on. Worse, we may try to find a source of the mysterious rhythm of its behaviour in the inner world of the spoon as it senses the world at each moment, and then acts out its ebbing and flowing cycle of behaviour for its own purposes. This is the error of focus without holism. Or, just as bad, we may locate the origin of this behaviour in some pervading rhythmic force acting on each spoon to give it its distinct behaviour. This is the error of holism without focus.

Mutual qualities of life can only be understood through seeing patterns with holism *and* focus – seeing how all things are contingent on each other.

Each transition in life increases the qualitative nature of both freedom and necessity. Matter uninformed by life follows the narrow paths of thermodynamic necessity; spoons have no alternatives except to swing in dynamic patterns of co-ordination. Life plays with the possibilities of energy and matter, creating forms that are precarious but always in living motion – obeying the physical laws but revealing new worlds of living freedoms within them. We humans have choices about how we connect and about which pattern to join. And in our creativity we bring into existence new qualities for patterning mutual life.

A quality is both something that we are and something that we can use – it is part of both our being and our doing. The patterns of the past brought us to this moment; in this moment we set up the patterning of the future.

In human life it is through works of our imagination that we bring forth new sources of abundance – music, art, tools, language, writing, money, the Web. Each sustains a mutual quality that allows us to live together within a new domain of infinite potential. Each individual must be nurtured into the qualities of shared life; they are only sustained through our universal creative integrity. Only if we all speak can any one of us be a speaker, and any one story speak to us all.

The island of Integrity

Integrity – the making and preservation of wholeness – links our inner world of purpose and intent with outer qualities of shared life. The first horizon of our daily lives is made up of the patterned integrities which we re-produce through our participation. The second and third horizons come into being as we step beyond these habitual routines and by our actions create new patterns of integrity which others can join.

We have a direct and intuitive sense of wholeness when we feel we are fulfilling the purpose of the pattern of which we are a part and are fully aligned with it. Take a moment to reflect on how you take part in any group or team social activity where you are aiming to contribute your best, making the whole all it can be. In those moments each of us experiences how, in realising myself, I manifest the whole, and realising the whole I manifest myself – the outer integrity of the pattern aligns with my inner sense of personal integrity.

In contrast, think of a situation where you keep a pattern going that conflicts with your sense of being true to yourself and of being right with the world. In each moment we make a judgement

about which patterns of integrity to support and renew, which to challenge, and which to bring into being.

We share one planet, as a global society of human kind and as a living environment. We need to bring our human patterns of life at every level back into positive relationship to this shared Earth and restore our sense of common ground. We find ourselves in patterns at every scale from our household, through shared communities, nations and regions, to the whole Earth. We need to expand our awareness to recover wholeness and express our integrity at every level of our one planet life.

As we learn more we come to understand how every level is linked to every other. Whether it is the winds that transport sand through the atmosphere from the Sahara to the Amazon, or the global retailer who transports goods from across the world to my door, every pattern links to every other for better or worse. Every pattern has its own scale and scope in time and space, and has its place in sustaining the integrity of the others. A choice at one level will reverberate through the others.

Every living thing, every pattern is constantly resolving the tension between being-as-itself and being-as-part-of-the whole. A living pattern depends on its participation in the shared abundance of which it is a part – an organism in its ecosystem, a household in its community, or a company in the marketplace. The larger whole supports the part, and the part renews the whole. The restoration of wholeness calls for us to maintain this expanded awareness of the patterns we are in and how they relate to the health and integrity of others.

This way of thinking inverts the habit of our conventional economics in which any cost or benefit of a market transaction that impacts a third party is thought of as an 'externality' lying beyond the parties to the transaction. No one has responsibility for it. We are now suffering the accumulated consequences of many negative externalities. Our human economies have built our wellbeing but are having negative and degenerative effects on the whole natural economy of which they are a part and on which they depend.

It is a deep irony that the extraordinary power of our market economies to create ever increasing variety and self-reinforcing abundance is simultaneously depleting the richness of the planetary ecosphere on which we all depend. We know that companies and societies must return profits to renew themselves, but we have chosen to ignore the wider patterns of renewal. If we mine the ecosphere instead of nourishing its living flows, sooner or later it will fail us.

What is true of the relationship between the human economy and the biosphere is equally true of the relationship between the many levels of human society. Everywhere we are struggling to sustain a sense of solidarity and integrity in societies, with many people feeling that global patterns are undermining rather than supporting their communities.

For us all to thrive we need to move beyond the notion of sustainability, which can often mean no more than reducing the rate of harm of human activities on the natural world, to a *regenerative* relationship, where households, communities, regions, and countries come back into nourishing and renewing each other and the living places they inhabit. Life has shown that regenerative abundance is open-ended over aeons; regenerative human civilisation is technically possible and is the only mode of long-term thriving available to us – we just need to shift from depletive and extractive patterns to restorative ones that grow with the flow of life. It looks hard from where we are standing in our long-established H1 patterns, but we belong here on this planet, and we can surely find ways to restore our own home.

As we seek a path back to global integrity of humankind with itself and the planet, we can take heart from our intuitive appreciation of the beauty of this planet and the life it has given us. When we walk through a woodland we are in the midst of vast complexity, but instead of being overwhelmed we are refreshed, everything within us resonates with the coherence of life and our place within it. If we bring that same intuition to bear to connect

us more deeply with the abundant potential of one planet living in every moment, it will not lead us astray.

A Compass for Navigation

To continue with the navigational metaphor, and to provide a simple, memorable structure, we can place these four islands at the four points of the compass.

The north-south pair of islands are like the axis of the Earth that we all share – they capture the fundamental dynamic reality of flows building shared structures of life at every scale. These are the patterns that connect. The compass encourages us to locate ourselves within these patterns of mutually reinforcing wholeness and abundance.

The east-west pair evoke the process by which life brings forth and embodies a world. The compass encourages us to locate ourselves in patterns of relationship with others adding to the variety and qualities of mutual life.

A compass has to be used where you are; it does not tell you the path ahead. It helps you bring your knowledge of where you have been into relationship with your goal so that you can make a step from the familiar into the new. It links your inner imagination into real world action where you are. The foundational practice we need in order to use our compass is to awaken our pattern awareness – our sense of holism as well as focus – as introduced at the start of this section.

The islands are prompts to deepen our awareness of the living world around us and thus to cultivate a fuller appreciation of the future potential of the present moment, rather than theories or models of the world. They are aids to awaken enquiry and deepen our perceptive understanding. The brushes and paints of an artist are not a model or theory of the yet-to-be-made painting, they are ways to bring the work of the imagination into relationship with the canvas to realise a unique creative expression of our humanity. Similarly, we can use these images to bring our full capacity for visionary future consciousness into practical action that is as wide open and as expressive of our whole persons as art. Treat these prompts as invitations to practise the unique artistry of your life, in a pattern of other lives, to realise the hope you hold.

The Patterning of Hope

We navigate in the third horizon by finding ways to improvise our stories together, however hard that might seem.

We have lived for a while with the myth of the invisible hand of the market, the idea that through our mutual exchange of the necessities of life we will prosper together and individually. It's not a bad idea but nor is it enough. It leaves out the view that looks on the other as part of the self, and our human society as part of our living planetary home.

To participate fully in our shared life is to experience hope even in the presence of death, that of others and ourselves, imminent or future. Every great tradition has told us again and again that to live is to participate in the flow with an open and loving heart; that through being-in-the-whole we become most fully being-for-ourselves; that this truth must be learned and lived out one life at a time on behalf of all.

New societies of life can tap into the open-ended abundance of the economy of experience. By the economy of experience I do not mean what this phrase usually means – ways to make a business out of the experience of others. I mean that the practice of mutual life reveals new creative possibilities for the experience of life itself.

We need to cultivate the invisible mind of the planet, learning to live skilfully together, where each act of intentional creation enriches every other.

Such a way will bring a new commerce to the abundance of goodwill and human potential that is ready to express itself and bring a rich life to all on the planet; it will be sustained by a new work of our collective imagination that will allow us to live abundantly amongst these imagined islands. If we serve the wholeness of life with hope in every moment, life will renew.

ACKNOWLEDGEMENTS

Although this book bears the name of only one author it is built with the ideas and experience of others.

Tony Hodgson has for many years been a close colleague and guide on my journey in futures work, and it was his formulation of three horizons that led directly to the practice reported here. Ian Page was an early partner in the further development of the ideas and made essential contributions to how we understood the ambiguity of the second horizon. Andrew Lyon, the Converger of the International Futures Forum, has brought rich first-hand experience to our understanding of the practice. Andrew Curry of The Futures Company has been a fellow traveller from the beginning and contributed his wide knowledge of futures work to the evolving ideas.

Graham Leicester, the Director of IFF, has been more responsible than anyone for bringing Three Horizons into widespread use through the many projects in which he has introduced it, several of which are reported here in his own words. He has also been my constant advisor in the production of this book, suggesting approaches to the structure, reviewing and improving the text, and in every way supporting my efforts.

There are many others with whom I have worked in IFF discussions who have informed my thinking in important ways, some in particular through a series of small IFF meetings that explored psychological capacity and hope in the context of futures work: Napier Collyns, Roanne Dods, Kate Ettinger, Margaret Hannah, Phil Hanlon, Maureen O'Hara, Neville Singh. With Martin Albrow I had very stimulating and useful discussions on integrity which suggested the direction for the ideas that matured into those in this book. Many others within IFF have been companions along the way.

I am particularly grateful to Jennifer Williams for her support and for the beautiful illustrations.

Andrew Carey at Triarchy Press has been an excellent and supportive editor, playing an essential role in shaping the final text.

Special thanks to my wife Ruth, who has done her best to reform my wayward prose and has helped me every step of the way.

Notes

Introduction

The first published version of a three horizons model was in the management book *The Alchemy of Growth* (Baghai, Coley *et al.* 2000). The idea of using the three horizons as three orientations to the future in the present was introduced at the Intelligent Infrastructure Futures project (Sharpe and Hodgson 2006) and (Hodgson and Sharpe 2007).

The evolution of the approach presented in this book, and its relationship to other futures techniques such as scenario planning, is described in (Curry, Hodgson *et al.* 2008) which provides a good list of references for those with a technical interest in the futures field.

See the Part III notes for references to examples and methods.

Part I: Three Horizons

Horizon 1 – Today's Dominant Pattern
Increasing returns and lock-in, see (Arthur 1989; Arthur 1990).

Horizon 2 – Ambiguous Innovation
The concept of disruptive innovation as used here is from (Christensen 1997).

The idea of H2 plus and minus was introduced by Ian Page (personal communication).

Part II: The Practice of Future Consciousness

Seeing Everything as Patterns
John Cage, Lecture on Nothing (Cage 1978).

The approach to understanding patterns and value used throughout the book is developed in more detail in (Sharpe 2010). In general, these ideas draw heavily on the background of enactive cognition and philosophy as first introduced by Francisco Varela (Maturana and Varela 1987; Varela, Thompson *et al.* 1993) and under development by a wide variety of researchers and philosophers (Stewart, Gapenne *et al.* 2010). The enactive framework provides a systematic way of moving between third-person description and first-person experience that lies at the heart of how I view the dual use of three horizons as descriptions of patterns and qualities of experience.

More generally, the concepts of enaction draw on the foundational philosophy of the mindfulness traditions and the concept of co-dependent origination as developed by Nagarjuna (Garfield 1995). I have tried throughout to use concepts in a way that is consistent with these foundations, though I may not always have succeeded.

Putting Ourselves in the Picture
Iona Heath's lecture is available at: www.bit.ly/3horizons12

This section, particularly the thoughts about 'learning to love uncertainty', is influenced by IFF's work on '21st century competencies' in (O'Hara and Leicester 2012).

On Disruptive Innovation, see (Christensen, 1997).

Convening the Future: from Mindsets to Perspectives
Tony Hodgson was the first to identify each horizon as an attitude to the other horizons, and this was elaborated into the full table by Ian Page (personal communication).

Part III: Journeys in Three Horizons

Carnegie Commission on Rural Community Development

The Commission's Charter for Rural Communities and related materials can be accessed at www.bit.ly/3horizons01

Transformative Innovation in Education

The full story of IFF's collaboration with Education Scotland to introduce Three Horizons into the Scottish education system is told in a short book (Leicester, *et al.* 2013 - second edition) which provides a full practical overview of the method, how it has been used, and how it has combined with other techniques and approaches (dilemma mapping, change tools) to promote transformative action. These resources, including a Three Horizons Kit for strategic conversation, are now accessible online at www.bit.ly/3horizons03

Winter Planning in NHS Fife

There is more information about the original Three Horizons process at: www.bit.ly/3horizons04

The SHINE project that arose from the Three Horizons analysis is described in more detail at: www.bit.ly/3horizons14

The links with Southcentral Foundation in Alaska which developed from it being identified as an element of 'third horizon practice in the present' are described at: www.bit.ly/3horizons06

Scottish Broadcasting Commission

The final report of the Scottish Broadcasting Commission, Platform for Success, is available at: www.bit.ly/3horizons07

Note that the report structure begins with a third horizon vision and then explicitly sets out a transition strategy to move through the switchover from analogue to digital in 2011 and beyond.

Southcentral Foundation, Alaska

More information about Southcentral Foundation can be found at www.bit.ly/3horizons08

The 'adjacent possible' concept is introduced by Kauffman (2002) to describe processes at the molecular level that are one step away from the actual. There are many ideas in his discussion that seem to have relevance for explorations of creative integrity and the discussion in Part IV of 'living into the future'.

Other Examples

Producing the Future: Understanding Watershed's Role in Ecosystems of Cultural Innovation (Leicester 2010).

Intelligent Infrastructure Futures, Technology Forward Look (Sharpe & Hodgson 2006).

Andrew Curry of has been a co-developer of Three Horizons with members of IFF and used it on a variety of projects: www.bit.ly/3horizons09

Part IV: The Patterning of Hope

Knowing and Living

David Bohm's essay *The Qualitative Infinity of Nature* (Bohm & Nichol 2003) makes clear how any conceptualisation of the universe is always limited in scope, and provides inspiration for this section and the formulation of the four imaginary islands, especially 'infinite variety'.

Viktor Frankl (Frankl 2011)

Ursula Le Guin on 'message' (Le Guin).

"You can only see it if you love it", Maureen O'Hara, personal communication.

The Power of the Powerless (Havel 2009).

Stepping into Future Consciousness

The story of Plenty Coups is told in *Radical Hope* (Lear 2009).

Hope

Malala Yousafzai speaking to the UN on the rights of all children to an education: www.bit.ly/3horizons10

Scottish schoolgirl Martha Payne's blog about her school dinners is at: www.bit.ly/3horizons11

Navigating on the Open Sea

Karen O'Brien, *Transformative Imagination*, public lecture, Moderna Museet, Stockholm, Sept 2019

Navigation with imaginary islands is described by Hutchins (1995) who uses (Riesenberg 1972) as his source.

Jane Jacobs (2000) provided me with much of the inspiration for the relationship between ecology and economy and in particular with the notion of how diversity expands through the diverse use of energy which I use in the rainforest island.

Janine Benyus (Benyus, 1997)

The discussion of integrity draws on (Hodgson 2011). It is also informed by the extensive work on regenerative design that may be found in the work of Mang & Haggard (2016) and Daniel Wahl (2016).

IFF has worked with Watershed in Bristol over several years to understand value and ways of organising that are not limited by the assumptions that underpin markets and money. The results of this work provide further reading on the economy of experience and how this relates to Three Horizons (Leicester 2010; Sharpe 2010).

BIBLIOGRAPHY

Arthur, W. B. (1989). 'Competing technologies, increasing returns, and lock-in by historical events', *Economic Journal* 99(394): 116-131

Arthur, W. B. (1990). 'Positive feedbacks in the economy', *Scientific American* 262(2): 92-99

Baghai, M., S. Coley, *et al.* (2000). *The Alchemy of Growth: Practical Insights for Building the Enduring Enterprise*, Da Capo Press

Benyus, J. M. (1997). *Biomimicry: Innovation inspired by nature:* Morrow

Bohm, D. & L. Nichol (2003). *The Essential David Bohm*, Routledge

Christensen, C. M. (1997). *The Innovator's Dilemma: When New Technologies Cause Great Firms to Fail*, Harvard Business School Press

Curry, A., Hodgson, A., *et al.* (2008). 'Seeing in Multiple Horizons: Connecting Futures to Strategy', *Journal of Futures Studies* **13**(1): 1-20.

Frankl, V. E. (2011). *Man's search for ultimate meaning*, Random House

Garfield, J. L. (1995). *The Fundamental Wisdom of the Middle Way: Nagarjuna's Mulamadhyamakakarika*, Oxford University Press

Havel, V., *et al.* (2009). *The Power of the Powerless: Citizens Against the State in Central-Eastern Europe*, Routledge

Hodgson, A. (2011). 'An Image of Global Integrity: The parameters of an enlightened global society', *Network Review*, (Spring). Available at: www.iffpraxis.com/wg-theory

Hodgson, A. & Sharpe, B. (2007). 'Deepening Futures with System Structure' in *Scenarios for Success: Turning Insight into Action* (Sharpe, B. and Van der Heijden, K., eds) Wiley

Hutchins, E. (1995). *Cognition in the Wild*, MIT Press

Jacobs, J. (2000). *The Nature of Economies*, Modern Library

Kauffman, S. A. (2002). *Investigations*, Oxford University Press

Le Guin, U. K. 'A Message about Messages', available at: www.ursulakleguinarchive.com/MessageAboutMessages

Lear, J. (2009). *Radical Hope: Ethics in the face of cultural devastation*, Harvard University Press

Leicester, G., Sharpe, B. (2010). *Producing the Future: Understanding Watershed's Role in Ecosystems of Cultural Innovation*, Watershed

Leicester, G. *et al.* (2013 - 2nd ed). *Transformative Innovation in Education: a playbook for pragmatic visionaries*, Trarchy Press

Mang, P. & Haggard, B. (2016). *Regenerative development and design: a framework for evolving sustainability*, Wiley

Maturana, H. R. and Varela, F. J. (1987). *The Tree of Knowledge: The Biological Roots of Human Understanding*, Shambhala

O'Hara, M. and Leicester, G. H. (2012). *Dancing at the Edge: competence, culture and organisation in the 21st century*, Triarchy Press

Riesenberg, S. (1972). 'The organization of navigational knowledge on Puluwat', *Journal of the Polynesian Society* 1(81): 19-55

Sharpe, B. (2010). *Economies of Life: Patterns of Health and Wealth*, Triarchy Press

Sharpe, B. & Hodgson, A. (2006). *Intelligent Infrastructure Futures: Technology Forward Look*, Foresight Directorate, UK Dept of Trade & Industry

Stewart, J., Gapenne, O., *et al.* (2010). *Enaction: toward a new paradigm for cognitive science*, MIT Press

Varela, F. J., Thompson, E., *et al.* (1993). *The embodied mind: cognitive science and human experience*, MIT Press

Wahl, D. (2016). *Designing Regenerative Cultures*: Triarchy Press

About the Author

Bill Sharpe is an independent researcher in science, technology and society. He was a research director at Hewlett Packard Laboratories where he led research into everyday applications of technology and introduced scenario methods to HP to support long-range research and innovation. Since leaving HP he has specialised in science, technology and policy studies for business strategy and public policy foresight.

With a background in psychology he is particularly interested in drawing on leading edge research in cognition and systems thinking to find new ways of tackling complex problems. He is a member of International Futures Forum and author of *Economies of Life: Patterns of Health and Wealth* (Triarchy Press, 2010).

About the Illustrator

Jennifer Williams is critically acclaimed at making hand-made books, cut outs, photographs, illustrations, prints and puppets.

She is a trustee and member of the International Futures Forum and for 31 years directed the Centre for Creative Communities.

International Futures Forum

International Futures Forum (IFF) is a non-profit organisation established to support a transformative response to complex and confounding challenges and to restore the capacity for effective action in today's powerful times.

At the heart of IFF is a deeply informed inter-disciplinary and international network of individuals from a range of backgrounds covering a wide range of diverse perspectives, countries and disciplines. The group meets as a learning community as often as possible, including in plenary session. And it seeks to apply its learning in practice. IFF takes on complex, messy, seemingly intractable issues - notably in the arenas of health, learning, governance and enterprise - where paradox, ambiguity and complexity characterise the landscape, where rapid change means yesterday's solution no longer works, where long-term needs require a long-term logic and where only genuine innovation has any chance of success.

www.internationalfuturesforum.com

About the Publisher

Triarchy Press is a small, independent publisher of books that bring a wider, systemic or contextual approach to many different areas of life, including:

Government, Education, Health and other public services
Ecology, Sustainability and Regenerative Cultures
Leading and Managing Organisations
The Money System
Psychotherapy and Arts and other Expressive Therapies
Walking, Psychogeography and Mythogeography
Movement and Somatics
Innovation
The Future and Future Studies

For books by Nora Bateson, Daniel Wahl, Russ Ackoff, Barry Oshry, John Seddon, Phil Smith, Bill Tate, Patricia Lustig, Sandra Reeve, Graham Leicester, Nelisha Wickremasinghe, Bill Sharpe, Alyson Hallett and other remarkable writers, please visit:

www.triarchypress.net